Before you read this book, please read the following three statements!

1. The entire message of this book must be dated from April, 1973. Many predictions of this vision have already been fulfilled, some will happen in the near future, and others in years to come. Please do not read this book with the expectation that all the calamities will happen overnight. I do believe that most of this vision will be fulfilled in our generation.

2. I do not intend for this vision to endorse any doctrinal position concerning The Great Tribulation. When I speak about persecution of Christians, I am not referring to the Tribulation. I refuse to be drawn into any arguments about when Christians will be evacuated from this earth at the return of Christ. This vision is not a doctrinal statement.

3. I repudiate the idea that this vision is a "fearmongering" message. Some will suggest this vision will only help to bring about some of the calamities and that you "get what you preach." I disagree completely. That logic would suggest Noah brought about the flood by warning about it. I have shared my vision and with this statement I will never again defend it. Its message can be tested only by time and events. God will be the judge and nothing my friends or enemies say can hinder me in my course to warn readers that these things be true.

DAVID WILKERSON

THE
VISION

DAVID WILKERSON

SPIRE BOOKS

FLEMING H. REVELL COMPANY ● Old Tappan, New Jersey

THE VISION

A SPIRE BOOK

Published by Pyramid Publications
for Fleming H. Revell Company

Eleventh printing November 1976

SPIRE BOOKS are published
by Fleming H. Revell Company
Old Tappan, New Jersey 07675, U.S.A.

CONTENTS

*". . . I was not disobedient
unto the heavenly vision."*

(Acts 26:19)

And the Lord answered me, and said, Write the vision, and make it plain upon tables, that he may run that readeth it.

For the vision is yet for an appointed time, but at the end it shall speak, and not lie: though it tarry, wait for it; because it will surely come, it will not tarry. (Habakkuk 2:2,3)

"... and in a trance I saw a vision ..."
(Peter in Acts 11:5)

"... and I was astonished at the vision ..."
(Daniel in Daniel 8:27)

"Now I am come to make thee understand what shall befall thy people in the latter days: for yet the vision is for many days."
(Daniel in Daniel 10:14)

INTRODUCTION

I have had but two visions in my lifetime. The first came to me in 1958, when a vision of God took me from a little town in Pennsylvania to New York City to work with teen gangs and drug addicts. That was not a false vision. Now, years later, its reality is shown by the youth centers spread all around the world. Gangs and addicts have not only been converted, but many are even preaching the gospel as ministers and missionaries.

A second vision came to me this summer (1973). It is a vision of five tragic calamities coming upon the earth. I saw no blinding lights, I heard no audible voices, nor did I hear from an angel. While I was in prayer late one night, these visions of world calamities came over me with such impact that I could do nothing but kneel, transfixed, and take it all in.

At first I did not want to believe what I saw and heard. The message of the vision was too frightening, too apocalyptic, too discomforting to my materialistic mind. But the vision came back to me, night after night. I couldn't shake it off. Deep in my heart I am convinced that this vision is from God, that it is true, and that it will come to pass. Yet this vision has caused me to do some very real heart-searching. I have been afraid that most people won't believe it, or that I'll be branded as some kind of fanatic. I shared this vision with some of my closest friends and associates and have been warned against publishing it. Who wants to listen to a message of economic confusion in a time of great affluence? Who wants to be told judgment is coming when so many can't even cope with life as it is? Who will ever believe that the religious freedom we now enjoy will soon be threatened and that a Jesus revolution will turn into a Jesus revulsion movement?

In spite of my fears and apprehensions, I can no longer shake off a conviction that this vision must be published. If I understand divine guidance at all, God has instructed me to speak out. I have tested the vision by the Word of God, and Scripture correlates its message. Parts of this vision will come to pass in the very near future. Some of the events are more distant. But I believe all the events mentioned will happen in this generation!

I believe we are already in the time the Bible refers to as "the beginnings of sorrows." This world faces tribulation of unbelievable proportions, and even now the Earth is reeling under the impact of the first sampling of God's wrath. It seems that nearly everybody is wondering what is happening to nature, to moral standards, and to society. I believe that what is happening now is supernatural and is out of the reach of man's control.

Many who read this book will find it easy to forget its message during these "breathing spells" of good times. It's hard to think of judgment when you are basking in the sun on a warm beach. Earthquakes, famines, floods, and other disasters seem so far away when you are racing across a lake in a high-powered speedboat. It's difficult to imagine hard and tragic times when money is flowing, when freedoms are taken for granted, and when TV comedies make life appear to be so free and easy.

Nevertheless, God warns of sudden disaster when all men are crying peace and safety. The flood of Noah's age came when men were eating, drinking, marrying, divorcing, and living high. The multitudes who mocked the "unbelievable vision" of this prophet were suddenly faced with the fury of God's wrath.

Before you put aside this vision as the ramblings of a fanatic, hear this! Suppose it is true? What if I have really heard from God? This vision could be the actual warning from God through a human being to a lazy, slumbering world. Remember, too, the Bible says:

> . . . in the last days . . . your young men shall see visions . . .

Then, friend, it is time to get ready. It is past

time to prepare. The hour is late and time is getting short. Read this book with an open heart; then get into the last chapter for the solution.

ECONOMIC CONFUSION 1

A Crash Is Coming — 1

There is worldwide economic confusion just ahead. In my vision, this is the clearest thing I have seen. Many praying people now share this very same vision.

Not only is the American dollar headed for deep trouble, but so are all other world currencies. I see total economic confusion striking Europe first and then affecting Japan, the United States, Canada, and all other nations shortly thereafter.

It is not really a depression I see coming—but a recession of such magnitude that it will affect the lifestyle of nearly every wage earner in America and around the world. Countries that now control huge amounts of Western currency are going to be in very deep trouble also. Arab countries will especially be hurt.

Without a doubt, there are lean years ahead full of monetary confusion and despair. How soon is not clear, but it is not far away. The world's greatest economists will be at a loss to explain the confusion, and an international crisis of fear will develop. A false economic boom will precede the recession—but it will be shortlived.

A Few Good Years to Prepare — 2

In spite of all the danger signs around us of impending economic disaster, the next few years (from 1973) will be among the most prosperous in the history of mankind. They will be fat and flourishing years. In spite of tight money policies, people will continue to spend freely. Sales will continue to break records and people will spend more than ever in modern history. Credit debt will become nearly uncontrollable.

I see, very clearly, just a few years of tremendous affluence and continuing economic prosperity. Church budgets will increase, wages will increase—missionary giving will also increase.

Inflation, costs, and wages will spiral higher and higher. There will be a few minor adjustments in prices, but world economy will become white-hot.

When I received this vision in April of 1973, I also received clear instructions from the Holy Spirit to believe God for sufficient finances to clear all debts of our organization other than necessary mortgages. The message I received from God was very clear and to the point. It was simply this:

There is great economic confusion coming and lean years lay just ahead. There will be a few short, fat, and flourishing years to prepare for the lean years. Work and pray to clear off all debts and get ready for drastic cuts in budget. The money will not be flowing as it was in the past and if you are free of debt, you'll be able to maintain your programs even in the difficult years. Don't panic—don't be afraid—just prepare for it and expect it!

Bankruptcies of Major Corporations — 3

I believe we are going to witness the bankruptcies of some of this nation's major and most popular corporations. I see tremendous difficulty arising for credit corporations. There are going to be many people unable to pay off their heavy obligations to major credit card companies, causing near-chaos.

Thousands of small businesses will also be forced into bankruptcies. Three, and possibly four, of the major religious denominations will be forced to operate with a skeleton organization due to a lack of funds. More than a few churches are going to go bankrupt and a number of independent missionary societies and church organizations are going to have to pull back. All but a few of the radio and television ministries will have to be abandoned.

Tight money will trigger a wave of uncertainty and fear. Those who have money will hold it in reserve.

The United States government is going to "over-react" to the confused economical developments.

I see a flurry of near-panic decisions being made by various government agencies—but these hasty efforts to shore up the economy will backfire.

The President of the United States will make one, and possibly two, national radio and TV appearances to reassure the nation that all is well, and that the best of economic times is just ahead. It will not work. People will distrust these statements, and their fears will lead to a revolution at the polls.

The auto industry is going to be hurt badly. Makers of recreational vehicles are going to get hit very hard. Appliance inventories will pile up, and sales will fall off drastically.

Almost every economic indicator will be gloomy. It will be spotty at first—but will eventually affect nearly all industry.

A Rush to the Country — 4

There will be a sudden rush to buy farms, ranches, and homes in the country. Thousands will attempt to flee from cities, hoping that a return to the land and nature will provide security. There will be a growing urge to "get away from it all"— and much money will be invested in land and acreage in rural areas by people who have secret dreams of raising their own food and cattle and of becoming self-supporting. The price of open rural land will continue to soar. Acreage within 100 miles of most major cities will skyrocket out of reach to all but syndicates.

Unions to Face Dilemma — 5

Unions will face new pressures not to strike. No longer will workers be able to afford to be out of work for even one week. The government is going to take a hard line against strikers, and striking union members will no longer be able to get food stamps and other benefits once allowed. Inflation will force a new crisis between labor and management, and strikes by union members in some areas will lead to a complete shutdown of plants and a total loss of jobs.

Labor leaders are also going to be caught up in this wave of economic confusion. Many are going to be at a loss as to what action they should take. They will face an almost impossible situation because they will not be able to afford a strike—and yet, at the same time, they will not be able to afford *not* to strike.

Long strikes could paralyze industry and add to growing economic confusion.

The details are not clear to me—but I see terrible union problems ahead. Labor peace is just a dream, and there is nothing but real trouble ahead.

We may soon experience the most devastating strikes of all times.

Those Who Do Not Prepare Are Going to Get Hurt — 6

People who spend recklessly and buy unneeded material things will suffer the most. Speculators face difficult times ahead, and a good number of big developers are going to be completely wiped out.

The greatest building boom of all time is still in the future—and the Bible predicts it will come. But before that—soon—the building industry is going to face many setbacks. Housing starts will level off. There is a terrible squeeze coming for the entire building industry. Ministers who build expensive buildings in the name of God, without a clear mandate, will be seriously hurt. Those who undertake ego trips, who get involved in huge projects involving large sums of money, and who have not moved in the perfect will of God will face financial disaster.

If a man has a clear mandate from God to build or move ahead—he should proceed. But let him be absolutely positive that he is moving ahead with clear and positive direction from God. Otherwise, the project will not survive, and he will go bankrupt.

It is not a time to go into debt. It is a time to prepare, a time to get clear and out from under heavy financial burdens.

When I first received this vision, I argued with myself that I dare not hinder the initiative and vision of people who want to do great things for God and who, in the process of doing them, must invest huge sums of money. I have known the satisfaction of building institutions to the glory of God. I have always preached faith and positive action, and I would never dare to advise a man or woman of God to draw back or delay when God had clearly given direction to move ahead.

But this vision is so clear to me that I must speak out. I sense a kind of divine obligation to warn ministers and church organizations to take a long, hard look at all expansion programs and projects that require large sums of money. There are some building programs that must be delayed or abandoned.

The time has come now for Christian organizations to become more people-conscious than building-conscious. Most of the growth in the lean years that lie ahead should be in the areas of people-to-people ministries. Without a doubt, many religious organizations are going to survive the lean years by paying only the interest on their huge loans. This will result in a constant hassle to raise money just to meet maintenance budgets, which will, in turn, cause missionary projects to suffer.

Not Even Gold Will Provide Security — 7

Gold prices are soaring, but those who are investing in this commodity, hoping to find security, are in for a tragic surprise. The price of gold is going to rise astronomically, but it will not be sustained over a long period of time. Silver will also become a very precious metal, and its price will go wild. But neither silver nor gold will offer real security. The fluctuating and uncertain value of gold and silver will be a part of the total picture of economic confusion that grips the world.

Believe it or not—even gold will not hold its value. Gold hoarders are going to get hurt—badly. This is one of the most significant predictions in this book.

A New World Monetary System — 8

There will develop a call for revamping all world monetary systems into one uniform system. And even though the dollar will appear to be gaining strength just before the coming major recession, a new crisis will develop that will shake the entire financial world. It will be years before faith in the American dollar will be restored.

I believe a revived Roman Empire will eventually become the power base for a super world leader who will arise to restore economic order. He will no doubt institute a worldwide "walking credit card" system. Invisible numbers will be implanted on the forehead and forearm, and only photoscope scanners will be able to detect the numbers. The numbers could be assigned in three stacks of six digits each. This "mark" would be required by all and no one could buy or sell without this invisibly tattooed number.

Some kind of a world credit system will develop and nations will be able to utilize blocks of credit.

Although a universal money system may be far off in the future, a world credit system between nations will soon develop, setting the framework for the future world monetary and trade system.

Be prepared to hear of world trade agreements "policed" by an international governing committee. Strict guidelines for international trade will develop and a "world market" will be closely monitored by big power interests.

To put it plainly—we will soon witness the development of a world trade policy, supervised by a super secretary invested with unprecedented powers by all nations involved in international trade.

Suicide by Overdose — 9

Economic setbacks and confusion will catch many unprepared for the consequences. Suicide will follow. There will not be a repetition of scenes so familiar during the Great Depression when businessmen committed suicide by jumping from windows. Nor will they be putting guns to their heads and pulling the triggers. The new method will be suicide by overdoses from sleeping pills and other chemical sedatives. This trend is already developing and will get worse. Some very well-known people in the business world are going to commit suicide through overdoses of narcotics.

Because so many wealthy businessmen have private physicians, the general public will not be informed about the manner of these "accidental" deaths. In many cases the cause of death will not be generally known, but suicide by overdose will become so widespread that hiding it will become impossible.

A Backlash Against Environmentalists and Ecologists — 10

The economic confusion that is coming will lead to a backlash against strictures imposed by environmentalists on the business community. The environmentalists have been well accepted and admired when they have dealt with generalities. But when they begin to affect the pocketbooks of the men and women of this nation, they will come into disrepute.

I see coming a tremendous backlash against ecologists and environmentalists, with experts speaking out against many of the findings of those in these agencies. On talk shows, in magazine articles, and in other public discussions, an undercurrent will develop against those who are warning about the dangers of pollution and those who advocate environmental control. It will become popular to debunk the findings of these committees and to speak out against the programs proposed by federal, state, and local environmentalists.

Environmentalist groups like the Sierra Club and others are going to come under severe criticism. They will be accused of hindering the development of our resources, and they will be blamed for the growing economic confusion. These groups will become the scapegoats for an energy crisis, meat and food shortages, and loss of jobs.

Believe it or not, the environmentalists and ecologists are going to be challenged, repudiated, and for the most part, rejected in days to come. Powerful forces are already at work to rally public sentiment against the far-reaching proposals of the new environmentalists.

Confusion for the "Positive Thinking" Preachers — 11

Those who preach that all success is the end result of positive thinking are going to discover that there is another side to the coin. Great losses, confusion, and reverses will shatter the thinking processes of many well-meaning people who falsely believe that their successes and economic well-being are the result of their own positive thinking.

Jesus Christ Himself was an advocate of right thinking. God states that He has not given us "the spirit of fear, but of love, power, and a sound mind." But many good men have become worshippers of the power of the mind. Those who preach positive thinking in line with the concepts of Bible teaching will be able to offer men truths that will sustain them through the coming crises. Those who have minimized the sovereignty of God and who have substituted mental attitudes for reformed hearts will be exposed as false teachers. Positive thinking, without godly living, offers no hope in time of world and personal crises.

Anyone can be an advocate of the power of positive thinking when economic conditions are favorable and all things are going well. But when things begin to fall apart and everything is going into reverse—and when supernatural intervention alone can help—it is then that the real truth will surface. The truth is that all the positive thinking in the world will not change the fact that we are going to have a major recession. No preacher, no philosopher, no author will be able to change the direction God has ordained.

More Riots and Demonstrations — 12

The rioting and demonstrating, the looting and unrest of the sixties are now history. But the riots are not over. Another wave is coming. This time I see Puerto Ricans, Cubans, and Mexicans deeply involved. The coming economic confusion will ignite another round of demonstrations, riots, and civil disorder.

Social aid programs are going to be cut back and curtailed, and minority groups are going to be affected the most. These cutbacks, along with the curtailment of many government projects, will cause widespread unemployment among these groups.

I have never once believed that we have seen the end of violence and bloodshed and rioting in our streets. I abhor it and pray that God will spare us. But more than ever I am convinced that the worst is yet to come.

Also, I see great riots coming to many major

cities in South America. In the next decade, South America will become a powder keg, exploding in all directions.

The United States to Be Blamed — 13

Although economic actions in Europe will trigger the coming recession, the United States will be blamed by most nations for what happens. France will become one of the most vicious anti-American nations in the world. Politicians and businessmen in Europe and Japan will place the blame on Washington and the American bankers.

Drastic troop withdrawals from Europe will cause even more confusion. Leaders of the European Common Market will capitalize on this anti-American sentiment to establish a firmer power base and grip on world trade. The world's economic power base will shift to Europe.

Recovery from Recession — 14

There may be a full recovery from the coming recession, and there may still be another cycle or two of fat and lean years. Only God Himself knows the future—I have received only a hazy glimpse beyond the next decade. I seem to see a picture of a partial and almost complete recovery from the coming recession—but the world economy will continue in confusion until the time of the Antichrist. From this day on, there will hang over the entire world a

sense of fear and uncertainty about future economic conditions. Never again in the history of the
world will there be a time of complete confidence
and trust in world economies. Every little boom
period will carry with it a strong threat of a bust.
Men's hearts will begin to fail them from fear after
they watch the devastating effects of crippled economies.

There will come a time in the future when men
will be obsessed with buying, selling, planting, marrying, and divorcing—but it will be a time of false
prosperity. The Bible predicts that in this time of
great false prosperity, Jesus Christ will appear in
the clouds to evacuate the Christian.

Beware: Hoarding Will Not Help — 15

It is not a time to hoard money, because it will
not provide real security. It is still possible that we
can face the time when even government-insured
savings will not be paid. The only real security is in
land. Money that is hoarded will disappear like
sand out of a bag with holes in it.

This is also a time when the Christian must pray
about his giving to the church and to missionary
causes. Every cent that is now given to God's work
must be given with a purpose. Indiscriminate giving
just to ease the conscience or to unload God's tithe
on the church will no longer be acceptable to the
Lord. Those who obey God's Word and give willing-
ly during the fat years will never have to beg for

bread during the lean years. Those who see the hard times coming and prepare are wise.

I have some advice for those who believe the message of this chapter. I believe the advice is from the Lord.

Don't buy anything unless it is needed. Avoid going into debt—at all, if possible. Sell or trade off all questionable holdings. No matter what sacrifice is involved, pay off as much debt as possible and get your cash flow needs down to a minimum.

Trim your budget and cut your staff down to the bone. Avoid piling up credit card bills. Credit card debt is extremely dangerous from now on.

Don't panic—just be very cautious. Get a good reliable car and stick with it. Don't anticipate trading it for a good, long while. Hold on to it!

By all means, do not cheat on God. Keep your books with Heaven well balanced. Your future security depends on it. Give as generously as possible to missions and to the support of legitimate church work. Give, and it shall be given back to you.

The message I have received for all true believers is:

> A prudent man foreseeth the evil, and hideth himself: but the simple pass on, and are punished. (Proverbs 27:12)

DRASTIC WEATHER CHANGES AND EARTHQUAKES 2

Drastic Weather Changes — 1

Drastic weather changes are breaking records around the world. Some experts believe it is caused by volcanic ash from the eruptions in Iceland now being carried by the jet stream in the troposphere. I personally believe that much of the drastic weather we are seeing throughout the world today can be explained up to this point by science.

In past centuries the world has witnessed devastating major earthquakes, killer heat waves, horrible floods, and all kinds of bizarre changes in the weather. All things have always returned to normal.

In my vision, I have seen very little that is supernatural about the drastic weather changes we have experienced up to this time. But I also see very clearly divine intervention about to happen throughout the world. This world had best prepare for weather changes that cannot be explained by any other word but "supernatural." The world is about to witness the beginnings of great sorrows brought about by history's most drastic weather changes, earthquakes, floods, terrible calamities— far surpassing anything ever yet witnessed.

Earthquakes Coming to the United States — 2

The United States is going to experience, in the not-too-distant future, the most tragic earthquake in its history. One day soon this nation will be reeling under the impact of the biggest news story of modern times. It will be coverage of the biggest, most disastrous earthquake in history.

It will cause widespread panic and fear. Without a doubt, it will become one of the most completely reported earthquakes ever. Television networks will suspend all programing and carry all-day coverage.

Another earthquake, possibly in Japan, may precede the one that I see coming here. There is not the slightest doubt in my mind about this forthcoming massive earthquake on our continent. I believe it will be many times more severe than the San Francisco quake.

I am not at all convinced that this earthquake will take place in California. In fact, I believe it is going to take place where it is least expected. This terrible earthquake may happen in an area that's not known as an earthquake belt. It will be so high on the Richter scale that it will trigger two other major earthquakes. I also believe we are going to see, later, a major earthquake in the Aleutian Islands, which will result in a number of smaller earthquakes and aftershocks all along the west coast of the United States.

Without a doubt, earthquakes are going to strike the United States and other parts of the world with growing intensity. Concern about earthquakes will be uppermost in forthcoming years. News about government scandals, news about war and even economic problems will be completely overshadowed by earthquakes. Within minutes after this quake hits, the whole country will know it, and millions will be stunned and shocked. Thousands will be affected with much loss of life and millions of dollars' worth of damage. Minor earthquakes, aftershocks, and tremors will be recorded almost daily throughout the world. Earthquakes will become the number one cause of fear and consternation.

The earth is actually going to shake, and there will be numerous other earthquakes in various places throughout the world. This is one kind of judgment that cannot be explained by the scientists. It is supernatural intervention into the affairs of men. It is an act of God causing havoc and judgment, calling men to repentance and reverence. It can strike at any time, and there is no way to deter it. Men will just have to stand back in awe and terror as the power of God is demonstrated in the earthquake.

I believe the recent earthquakes in Nicaragua and Mexico were a warning from Heaven that this is just the beginning. Seismic laboratories are even now recording tremors and aftershocks almost daily around the world.

Famine Is Coming — 3

Famine is coming to the world in our generation, and millions will die of starvation. Catastrophic years lie just ahead, with drought, floods, and other weather disasters wiping out great amounts of the world's food production.

Snowless winters will bring dismal crop production and famine conditions in central and western Russia. India, Pakistan, all of southeast Asia, and Africa will be especially hard hit.

The forty-month drought in Africa and the prolonged dry spell in Brazil will both end temporarily. There will be some relief, but conditions will worsen. In Africa, millions will face starvation.

American food reserves will dwindle—partially due to drought and floods in this country. Wheat, rice, and soybean reserves will be completely exhausted. The demand for corn, rice, and wheat will not be met.

The world, in our own generation, will face the frightening prospect of world population growing much faster than the food supply. We are already too far back to catch up.

The world has faced famine and drought before —but there is a difference this time. In years past, the world recovered when good harvests came in.

Now—we cannot recover! We have already had too many bad years, and the worst is yet to come. The situation will only worsen. And, because of overpopulation, we will never catch up.

This is, without a doubt, the last-day world famine predicted by God's Holy Word in the book of Joel.

Alas, this terrible day of punishment is on the way. Destruction from the Almighty is almost here! Our food will disappear before our eyes; all joy and gladness will be ended in the Temple of our God. The seed rots in the ground; the barns and granaries are empty; the grain has dried up in the fields. The cattle groan with hunger; the herds stand perplexed for there is no pasture for them; the sheep bleat in misery.

Lord, help us! For the heat has withered the pastures and burned up all the trees. Even the wild animals cry to you for help, for there is no water for them. The creeks are dry and the pastures are scorched.
(Joel 1:15-20, *The Living Bible*)

The Beginnings of Sorrows — 4

Floods, hurricanes, tornadoes, and hailstorms will occur more frequently. More than one-third of the United States will be designated a disaster area within the next few years.

Men will be talking about nature being "out of control." Strange happenings in nature will baffle scientists. Earth eruptions, blood and moon haze, strange signs in the heavens such as cosmic storms —these and other events never before seen will cause many to wonder. The haze hanging in the cosmos will turn the moon red and will cause periods of darkness over the earth—almost as though the sun refused to shine.

Nature Will "Go Wild" — 5

Nature will unleash its fury with increasing intensity over the next decade. There will be short periods of relief, but almost every day mankind will witness the wrath of nature somewhere in the world. These record-breaking changes will be above and beyond anything experienced in the past.

Floods, hurricanes, and tornadoes will destroy crops, animals, and much wildlife, driving prices even higher and causing some experts to suggest that nature is losing its balance.

Weather will become increasingly difficult to forecast. Sudden storms will appear without warning. Southernmost regions will be gripped by record cold waves and northern areas will experience record heat waves.

There will be periods of relief when men will say, "Things continue as they were from the very foundation of the earth. There is nothing unusual about what is happening, so be at ease."

Discerning people will have within them an innate knowledge that God is behind these strange events and is unleashing the fury of nature to force men into a mood of concern about eternal values. These violent reactions of nature will clearly be orchestrated by God to warn mankind of the coming days of wrath and judgment. It is almost as though all heaven is crying out, "Oh Earth, heed His call. He holds the pillars of Earth in His hands. He will shake the Earth until His voice is heard. He rides King of the flood and Lord of the winds and rains."

Mankind will yearn for a return to normal conditions, but the time is coming when there will be no return. God has aroused Himself as one who awakens from sleep, and His anger is kindled toward stubborn and sinful men. He will eventually melt the very elements with fervent heat, but until that last hour when this earth shall pass away, God will pour out His vials of wrath. The God of nature will use His judgments to reveal His power in warning mankind to flee from His wrath.

Short Periods of Relief — 6

Many men will appear to be repentant during the times of violent chastisement by nature, but the short periods of relief will make it appear that nature has "settled down," and men will be comforted by warmth, sunshine, and normal seasonal weather. But more violence, far worse, will soon follow.

Airline pilots will be reporting the worst flying conditions in aviation history. The most intense hurricanes are coming. Many parts of the world face the most violent winters of all times. Europe faces the worst winter lashings ever.

Depletion of Relief Funds — 7

Relief and disaster funds will become nearly depleted. Insurance companies will face huge losses. Many farmers will face financial disaster.

Earthquake damages alone will drain and deplete nearly all disaster funds. And there is a limit to what national governments can afford. Unlimited funds are not available, and the peoples of each nation will soon learn there will be no one left to turn to but God.

Americans will be shocked to learn that disaster funds are exhausted. A rude awakening is coming in this area.

Outbreaks of Epidemics — 8

In the aftermath of famine, floods, and earthquakes, mankind faces the threat of new epidemics. There will be a major cholera epidemic sweeping through various underdeveloped countries. India and Pakistan face the threat of untold thousands dying from epidemics and starvation. Malnutrition, starvation, and all epidemics that accompany it will be a problem faced by a number of other nations as well. Food and relief supplies will not be adequate to combat these overwhelming problems, and many will die without help. Medical supplies will reach only a small proportion of those in critical need.

This will prove to be mankind's biggest war. It will be a war of nature against man. And although God promises never to abandon mankind, it will appear as though He has done so.

Hailstorms — 9

The drastic weather changes that are coming in the next decade will bring with them violent hailstorms of unbelievable proportions. Large chunks of ice will fall from the sky and cause much damage. These storms will not only destroy crops and smash automobiles, but they will also cause the death of many people.

Watch for reports of intense ice storms and hailstorms in the future. Also, prepare for the most severe winters of all time and record snowfalls in the United States and Canada.

For the past three years, records show that hailstorms have grown extremely worse, with larger and larger hailstones falling. The size of falling hailstones will become almost unbelievable.

Strange Signs in the Heavens — 10

The Bible predicts that in the last days unusual signs will appear in the heavens—blood, fire, vapors of smoke. I do not know the full significance of what Joel saw in his vision, but I do know that what I have seen reinforces every one of those predictions. There will appear strange and baffling signs in the heavens and stars. Many prophets over the centuries have seen visions of a huge comet colliding with the earth, spreading a blood-red kind of pollution over lakes, streams, and oceans and causing unusual signs to appear above.

I have seen no new revelation and I can find no Scripture to corroborate the vision of colliding planets. But what I have seen and can freely share is that the Holy Spirit confirms to my heart that the predictions of the prophet Joel will actually be seen and experienced by this generation.

I believe the prophets either saw cosmic storms of such magnitude that they appeared to earth people as balls of fire blazing through the sky, leaving behind a vaporlike trail—or a rain of falling stars or comets racing through earth's atmosphere.

The Decade of Disaster — 11

When will all of these things take place? Can intelligent men with rational minds accept the idea of an angry God pouring out wrath upon the earth because of sin and corruption? Will we actually live to see the day that civilized people sit in front of a television set and see the news coverage of disastrous earthquakes that claim the lives of multiplied thousands, or will there be a return to normalcy? Can we pass over all the present drastic weather changes as being nothing more than a cycle which the world is going through? After all, scientists can point out disasters two or three hundred years ago that are as tragic as anything described in this book.

I believe we have passed the point of no return. Almost every weather forecaster has added to his vocabulary words like "unbelievable," "what's happening?", "record-breaking," "strange," "fantastic," "unpredictable," "unseasonal," "unexpected," and "unusual."

Honest men everywhere have a growing feeling that somebody, somewhere, is tinkering with nature. And, though most people expect normal conditions to return soon, others, like me, are fully convinced that we have seen only the beginning of unpredictable, strange weather and coming disasters.

When and Why? — 12

I do not know when all of these things will happen. They will not all happen simultaneously. These vials of wrath that God will pour upon the earth will be orchestrated by God's supernatural hand. All that I am really sure of is that the Holy Spirit has prompted me to warn everyone who will listen that these things are coming and conditions will worsen.

Some of the predictions in this particular part of my vision will happen within the next few years. Other disasters predicted are still future but will surely come. Of one thing you can be very sure— there will be nothing but an overall worsening of weather conditions, an increase in earthquakes, un-explainable disasters with only short periods of relief. That I know to be the truth!

A FLOOD OF FILTH 3

A Moral Landslide Is Coming — 1

Woe unto all the inhabitants of the earth and sea, for the devil has come down to you with great wrath to deceive, if it were possible, even the elect and chosen of God. And how will Satan attempt to vex and deceive even God's chosen people? I believe he will attempt to reach his goal of seducing mankind by creating a moral landslide. He will open the floodgates of hell and seek to baptize the world in erotic filth, smut, and sensuality.

This moral landslide will surpass anything the human mind can conjure. Already a demonic spirit of lust is sweeping over many nations, bringing with it nudity, perversion, and a flood of filth.

A Dirt Bath — 2

This world faces a dirt bath so intense that it will vex the minds and souls of some of the most devout Christians alive today. The Bible says Lot vexed his soul night and day by the things he saw and heard in Sodom. Christians are soon going to be exposed to such violent filth and sensuality that it will take a firm grip on God to survive. Those on the fence are going to fall flat on their faces. Those who do not enter into the ark of God's safety are going to be swept away by this flood of filth.

Toplessness on Television — 3

Major TV networks will get caught up in this moral landslide. I predict that network programs will soon attempt bare-breasted scenes. Toplessness will be the new fad of those trying to liberalize the media. When the first response of "alarm" at this topless attempt dies down, full nudity will follow. It will be done "tastefully" at first, but when the artistic community joins in a chorus of praise for this "breakthrough" in media freedom, the floodgates will be open and then anything will go. Even certain clergymen will applaud nudity on TV and will try to explain it as a healthy development but little will be actually done to stop it. Surprisingly, those who speak out against it effectively will not be ministers and those known as devout Christians —rather, they will be certain Hollywood celebrities and TV personalities.

Triple-X-Rated Movies on TV After Midnight — 4

Be warned—In the not-too-distant future, the most wicked, X-rated porno movies will be shown on select cable networks after midnight. Cable television is already the favorite target of pushers of porno films.

In a few major cities in the United States, Canada, and Europe, triple-X-rated porno movies are already being shown. These movies are direct from porno producers in Sweden, Denmark, and the United States. These vile films feature total nudity, sexual intercourse, homosexuality, animal perversion, and sadism.

People will pay to have these erotic movies piped directly into their living rooms. If left unguarded, little children can switch on a knob and be exposed to the vilest kind of sexual perversion.

These porno movies will become so perverted and vile that even the most liberal atheist will blush and begin to complain. Along with exploitation of every sex theme, there will be emphasis on blood, violence, and occult practices. Demons, devils, and witchcraft will be glorified. The newest kind of sex deviation will be intercourse between demons and humans. These dramatic presentations will depict the devil as the father of sexuality.

Also featured will be movies glamorizing rape,

suicide, and mass sex violence—ending in death as the ultimate trip.

The new big thing in porno movies will be so-called "documentaries" of mass homosexual and thrill murders. They will be advertised as legitimate re-enactments, but will in actuality be nothing but unadulterated smut!

Sex and murder; sex and death; sex and blood; sex and torture; sex and violence—these are the themes of nearly all forthcoming porno films.

We are not far away from the time when R-rated movies will be showing in prime time on network. Porno movies on cable television will become so popular and so much in demand that the major networks will try to compete by showing films with as much sex and violence as they can show within legal limits.

Pleasure Palaces — 5

A growing number of motels will advertise themselves as "pleasure palaces." For just a few extra dollars, guests can have the latest triple-X-rated movies piped directly by video into their rooms. It will no longer be necessary for "decent" people to go into a slum-type, dirty theater to see the latest filthy porno movies. Instead, they will go to a beautiful motel and have a private showing all to themselves. This will become very popular among high school and college students, who will get groups together for porno parties in motel rooms.

Also available will be the same triple-X-rated video tapes for private home use. These video tapes can be played on any TV set with an electronic attachment. Porno parties will become a popular pastime of suburbanites.

Sex on the Newsstand — 6

Thousands of newsstands across the nation will soon be selling explicit sex magazines that will make *Playboy* seem almost puritanical. These magazines will be purchased even by pre-teens and will display full-color nudity and every kind of sex act.

There will be a flood of magazines designed especially to attract the female market, featuring male nudes. Even the most respected national magazines will become more erotic in their advertising and in their copy.

Much of the forthcoming pornography will feature a mixture of sexual perversion and occult practices in an effort to attract people who have "seen it all." Some of these porno magazines on the local newsstands will even glorify rape, child molestation, and murder.

Nearly every major city in the United States and Europe already had newsstands and porno shops featuring these very kinds of books. But soon it will be so widespread that the same material can be purchased at the local discount and drugstores.

Seducers, pornographers, and evil-minded men are going to show disdain for laws and local authorities. They will brazenly push their smut, filth, and pornography. They will open numerous massage parlors, peep shows, and "model" studios. If forced to close down temporarily, they will return again and again with smut even worse than before.

Sex Education to Get in on the Act — 7

Sex education classes in senior high school and college will feature the sex act on film. The diagrams now being used will be animated. I predict that the time is not far off when senior high school and college students will be exposed to sex education films featuring sexual foreplay and intercourse. They will be advertised as being "very tastefully done" by professionals.

Students will be told that homosexual love is normal and that sex acts between unmarrieds is desirable—"if each has a high regard for the other."

Watch for "cartoon sex" to become the next "innovation" in school sex education. Very tame and innocent at first, these cartoon-type educational films will become steadily more explicit and erotic.

A Temporary Setback for Smut — 8

Just prior to this moral landslide will come a short-lived movement by conservatives against smut and pornography. It will almost appear to be a national movement, gaining momentum as the courts, civic groups, churches, and government leaders join in an effort to stop this moral landslide. The courts will enact a few laws that seem favorable to anti-smut forces.

There will be a lot of talk about "cleaning up" television and newsstands. Articles will appear quite frequently in newspapers and magazines about valiant efforts to fight off the invasion of smut and pornography. There will be a few temporary victories in isolated places, but these victories will be short-lived. A few radio ministers will openly campaign against smut—but enthusiasm and support will soon wane.

Professional smut dealers and pornographers are not going to lie down and give up. They are going to test every law of the land, and they are going to find loopholes and ways and means to push their products. The clean-up campaign in the United States and overseas will not be successful. It will be a shortlived crusade, and a flood of filth will follow.

It is said that the pendulum swings from one extreme to the other. Many have been saying optimistically that we have had all the nudity, filth, and smut the nation can stand, and that the pendulum is about to swing the other way. Everything within me wishes that this could be so. But I fully believe that the flood of filth I have seen coming is the same kind of flood spoken of by the prophet Nahum.

> Behold I am against thee, saith the Lord of hosts; and I will discover thy skirts upon thy face, and I will shew the nations thy nakedness, and the kingdoms thy shame. And I will cast abominable filth upon thee, and make thee vile, and will set thee as a gazingstock. (Nahum 3:5,6)

The Sin of Sodom Is Coming — 9

The sin of Sodom will again be repeated in our generation. Of all the sins Sodom was guilty of, the most grievous of all were the homosexual attacks by angry Sodomite mobs attempting to molest innocent people.

Mass murders have become commonplace in our generation. We witnessed the television news coverage of the Olympic massacre. Mass murder sprees have become so frequent that they are now almost taken for granted. The world is no longer shocked by these tragedies as in the past.

The Bible says: "As it was in the days of Lot, so shall it also be in the days of the coming of the Son of Man." I have seen things in my vision which make me fear for the future of our children. I speak of wild, roving mobs of homosexual men publicly assaulting innocent people in parks, on the streets, and in secret places. These attacks by Sodomite mobs are certain to come, and, although they may not be publicized as such, those in the law-enforcement circles will know the full extent of what is happening.

A Homosexual Epidemic — 10

There are only two forces that hold back homosexuals from giving themselves over completely to their sin, and they are rejection by society and the repudiation and teachings of the church. When society no longer rejects their sin as abnormal and fully accepts them and encourages them in their abnormality, and when the church no longer preaches against it as sin and consoles them in their sexual activities—there no longer exist any hindering forces. The floodgates are open, and homosexuals are encouraged to continue in their sin. In my vision, I have seen these two roadblocks being swept away. When that which hinders is taken away, chaos will follow.

Believe me when I tell you the time is not far off that you will pick up your local newspaper and read sordid accounts of innocent children being attacked by wild homosexual mobs in parks and on city streets. The mass rapes will come just as surely as predicted in the Gospels. I see them coming in our generation.

Twenty-seven boys were murdered in Houston, Texas, by a small homosexual gang. This sordid news story is the beginning of many other such tragic outbreaks.

You can expect more than one homosexual scandal in very high places. The homosexual community will become so militant and brazen that they will flaunt their sin on network talk shows very shortly.

Very clearly, I see homosexuals coming out in mass numbers and deviate sex crimes becoming more numerous and vicious.

A Falling Away — 11

Moral standards among many church people will be shattered. Husband- and wife-swapping will be on the increase, and great numbers of young people will simply live together without getting married.

A constant barrage of sex and nudity by all the media will vex the minds and souls of the most devout children of Christ. It will cause the love of many to grow cold. It will lead to carelessness and faithlessness. It will be the major cause of a great "falling away." Those who stand against this flood of filth will be few, and they will be looked upon as "out of step" with an enlightened society and a more relevant church.

Easy abortion, the pill, and a growing sexual permissiveness will contribute to a revolution of immorality which will finally end in a baptism of filth so widespread that the human mind will be unable to take it all in.

Lovers of sensuous pleasures will far outnumber the lovers of God. Be aware and be warned—this is a full-scale war against God's chosen.

Sexual Immorality in the Ministry — 12

Divorce and immorality will be more and more commonplace among ministers. A growing number of priests will be involved in sexual affairs and will leave the priesthood. Others will continue in the priesthood but will carry on secret affairs. An ever-increasing number of Protestant ministers are going to "fall" into sexual sin, much of it carried on secretly.

I believe that even certain evangelical denominations will soon grant credentials to divorced ministers. Divorce among ministers will no longer carry a stigma. Church denominations will continue to "review" their opposition to divorce and will become more lenient with every new convention and conference. There is coming a "softening" toward divorce in churches and in the ministry. This is a trend that will not be stopped, even though the changes in attitude develop slowly.

I have had a curtain pulled back and, as it were, a vision of what is happening secretly to thousands of ministers and very devout people. Beneath all the piety and behind all the false fronts are secret affairs being carried on, hidden from the eyes of men. Among them are some of the most devout and well-known. Some very "religious" men and women are cheating and indulging in secret sex sins. They deplore their sin and they know it can never be accepted as right, but they seem powerless to withstand the force of this personal moral landslide. Unless they are extricated miraculously, it will lead to shipwreck and disaster for many homes and churches.

I see coming a day when every true minister and priest of the gospel will face his greatest hour of temptation. Those who thought they were beyond temptation will be tempted the most severely. God will keep and deliver those who turn to Him with all their hearts. Those who continue to flirt and indulge face a terrible hour of despair and failure. God will soon deal with secret sin with such fury that His judgments will begin to fall on the right and on the left in the lives of those who persist in their sins. Those who forsake secret sex sins will be renewed and healed.

What I have heard and seen is an urgent message from God's throne room—"There is sin in the camp and it must be purged." The hour has come when God will lay the ax at the root. He will cleanse His house and will sanctify His vessels for service in this midnight hour.

A Last-Ditch Attempt to Deceive God's Chosen — 13

I have seen the Jesus people of this generation as the "last Christian." Satan is going to come as an angel of light so subtle, innocent, and indefinable that few will recognize what is happening to them. He is going to camouflage his activities and attempt to deceive Christians with temptations that are legitimate within themselves—but that, when misused, become damning.

The number one temptation for the last Christian will be prosperity. The Bible warns that in the last days many Christians will be halfhearted, rich, prosperous, and in need of nothing. There is nothing evil or sinful in being prosperous and successful. Most of the patriarchs in the Bible were wealthy men. Abraham was very rich in cattle, in silver, and in gold. Job was immensely wealthy, owning 7,000 sheep, 3,000 camels, 500 teams of oxen, 500 female donkeys, and had many servants and a great house. God certainly is not against wealth and prosperity, because the Bible says he "hath pleasure in the prosperity of his servants" (Psalms 35:27).

However, I see millions of Christians being deceived by prosperity. The last Christian is going to be afflicted by prosperity and tested by it more than through poverty.

In my vision, I see Satan appearing before God one last time, as he did to accuse Job in the Bible. But this time he comes to ask permission to tempt the last Christian. Here is what I see:

> And the Lord said unto Satan, Where have you come from? Satan answered, From going to and fro in the earth and observing the last Christian. And the Lord said unto Satan, Have you considered these last-day Christians—how dedicated, how upright, how God-fearing, and Christ-loving they are? How they try to run from your evil plots? Then Satan answered the Lord, Yes, but just take away the hedge You've built around them. Job wouldn't forsake You in his poverty—but just increase and bless all the last Christians far beyond anything Job ever had and then see what happens. Make all these last Christians affluent like Job. Build them fancy new homes—give them fine automobiles—all the money and gadgets they need. Swamp them with

campers, boats, world travel, fine clothes, exotic foods, land holdings, and savings accounts. See what happens to your last Christians when they become full, rich, increased with goods, and are in need of nothing. They will forsake God and become self-centered.

I see automobiles, clothes, motorcycles, and all kinds of materialism becoming a bigger hindrance to the Christian than drugs, sex, or alcohol. I see thousands of Christians attached to and obsessed by things. They are so wrapped up in materialism that they become lukewarm, blind, weak, and spiritually naked. Yet in the midst of all their materialism, they are miserable and totally dissatisfied.

In my vision I see Satan standing back and laughing with glee:

Look at all the money-mad Christians— all the clothes hogs! Bitten by the security bug! Making heaps of money! Buying all new furniture! Getting bigger cars! Buying two or three of them! Buying, planting, selling, marrying, and divorcing! It ruined Lot's generation. And it will get you, too.

Look at all the well-paid, easy-living, big-eating Christians getting lazy, lukewarm, and becoming easy prey. God—pour it on them. It's getting to a lot of them, and it's making my job easier.

The God who owns the cattle of a thousand hills wants nothing that man owns. Not his house, car, clothes, speedboat, or surfboard. He wants only first place in the hearts of those who call themselves by His name.

Holy Ghost Swingers — 14

I see many of the last Christians who were once lovers of God becoming shipwrecked by their obsessive love for pleasure. Lovers of God find no pleasure in drugs, illegitimate sex, alcohol, tobacco, or smut. The devil knows that. Most of these fleshly pleasures offend and repulse the Christian. I see thousands of Christians sitting in theaters exposing themselves to degrading influences they once abhorred. They have not given themselves over to any particular sin, but they have become very comfortable in their addiction to off-color movies, numerous parties, socials, and wine-tasting. They really love God, but they love their pleasures even more. They are not really sinners before God—just strangers to Him. They have become so busy swinging and trying to live a liberated Christian life that they have changed drastically without knowing what they have become.

The sudden evacuation of Christians from the earth will catch many of them unawares. They have become socialized gadabouts who can't find one hour any more to talk to God in a secret closet of prayer.

I see the sin of the future as the misuse of leisure time. This has nothing to do with weeks spent on vacation. It's not the time spent touring Europe or

the Holy Land. It's not a hunting or fishing trip.
It's not hours spent surfing, boating, water skiing,
or horseback riding. These things are all legitimate
and good in themselves. I am talking about all the
wasted time. The time that a man has for himself to
choose what he will do with. Time that could be
spent in reading God's Word. Time that could be
spent in the secret closet talking to the Heavenly
Father.

I see Satan coming again to accuse the last
Christian:

> Look at the last-day Christian, the televi-
> sion addict! Look at him—hours and hours
> for soap operas, comedies, sports—but no
> time to get alone with God. He turns God
> off with a dial. He hunts, fishes, travels;
> plays golf, tennis, and basketball. He goes
> to movies and parties, and has become a
> gadabout, but he has no time to read his
> Bible or pray. Is this the last-day Christian
> who is supposed to walk by faith? Is this
> the one whose faith will overcome the
> world? Is this the one who is to prepare
> for a coming day of persecution and world
> chaos? Are these the playboy Christians
> upon whom the ends of the world will fall?

The greatest sin of the future against God is not
abusing the body, indulging the flesh, or even curs-
ing His name. The greatest sin against God now is
simply to ignore Him in a day and age in which He
is calling so clearly. I see an ironic development.
The last Christian, who lives so much closer to the

return of Christ than the early Christians, spends the least time of all in His presence.

The message of coming judgment and the return of Jesus Christ will not register with so many Christians for the same reason that the message and the pending doom did not get through to Noah's generation—because they were so in love with the pleasures of buying, selling, planting, and love-making.

A Gossip War — 15

I know now that Satan has declared war on every true minister of Jesus Christ. He will leave no stone unturned in an attempt to discredit and shipwreck every man of God who is determined to stay true. Those ministers and priests who refuse to cheat on their wives, who refuse to indulge in the freedom of the new morality, are going to be the target of the most vicious gossip of all times. Satan is going to raise up "gossip mongers" to harass, malign, and lie against them.

I believe that Billy Graham and other great gospel ministers throughout the world are going to face more and more ridicule, gossip, and misunderstanding by the press and by liberal people in the media. Every motive will be questioned and suspected. Every statement will be examined and cross-examined.

Ministers who thought they had no enemies in the world will wake up to discover that someone is talking about them. Pastors of churches are going to face the most malicious gossip of all. Innuendoes, lies, and false statements that will be floating around will come from the very pits of Hell.

It will be a supernatural demonstration of demonic powers. Not a single true minister of the gospel will be immune. The wives of ministers who are married will also come under attack.

Legions of lying spirits have been turned loose upon the world with the single purpose of accusing Christians through gossip and slander. This gossip war will not only be aimed against ministers of the gospel—but against all true believers of Jesus Christ, of all colors and creeds.

An Increase of False Doctrines — 16

Men will prefer false doctrines and new ideas rather than the truth of God's Holy Word. They will crowd around teachers who will give "new thoughts and revelations." Men and women will turn to the prophecies and teachings of men rather than giving heed to the doctrines of truth. They will give heed to seducing spirits and doctrines of devils.

We face an hour of gospel extremes, wherein seeking men who have itching ears will follow after ministers who appear as "angels of light," but who are in reality preaching and teaching heresy. The new doctrines will use the name of Jesus freely and will be ornamented with trappings of asceticism, self-denial, and willpower.

A fear of demon possession will grip many sincere

Christians. They will turn to teachers who speak more often of the power of Satan than they do of the power of God. I have seen, however, that this movement toward a fear of Satan within the church will be short-lived. Those who continue in an emphasis of Satanic possession of Christians will return to the old law and a life of works. Also, growing numbers of sincere Christians will sell everything and join Christian-type communes that feature monastery-type living and a set of laws by which to approach God.

A Phony Jesus Movement — 17

There will arise a movement of false "Jesus people" who will emphasize the casting out of devils. They will claim to heal the sick and do apparent wonders. They will be involved in feeding the poor and preaching great love. But among them are false prophets who have never surrendered all to Christ. They are those who preach love in His name, but who continue in their old sins and rebellion. They are workers of iniquity who are tools of Satan to discredit the true Jesus movement.

The Bible predicts that many of these false Jesus people will stand before God's throne saying—

Lord, Lord, have we not prophesied in thy name? and in thy name have cast out devils? and in thy name done many wonderful works? (Matthew 7:22 KJV)

But the Lord will say to them,

I never knew you: depart from me, ye
that work iniquity. (Matthew 7:23 KJV)

I believe this refers to those false Jesus people
who went about preaching in His name, operating
crash pads for runaway kids, feeding the poor and
clothing the naked—all in the name of Christ's
love, but without living the crucified, surrendered,
and resurrected life of Jesus. They whitewashed
their sins and added Jesus on top of it all. They
were joy-popping and tripping on Jesus, but had
never been to Calvary to have their sins washed
away.

When the hour of persecution comes, they will
return to their sex and drugs and old way of life.
Only those fully surrendered to Jesus Christ and
cleansed by His blood will survive.

Rebirth of the True Jesus Movement — 18

Suffering persecution and aware of the signs of
the times, an army of true Jesus followers will continue to arise like commandos. They will be a part
of an underground church that will be found
preaching the return of Christ and the end of the
age! They will be like a thorn in the side of the har-
lot church, and they will sting and sear the con-
sciences of men by their devotion and spiritual
power. Devil worshippers will be in open conflict
with all these true Jesus followers. Only those living by true faith will be able to discern the "spiritual wickedness" in high places.

"I Hate My Parents" — 1

The number one youth problem of the future will be *hatred of parents*. The world is soon going to be shocked by thousands upon thousands of teen-agers who confess, "I hate my parents."

We are now entering that period when a man's worst enemies will be members of his own household—father against son, mother against daughter, and in-laws hating one another. A teen-ager's biggest problem will be how to live with his parents.

Already, that parental hatred is spreading like cancer all over the world. Teen-agers who are forced to live with hypocritical parents are learning to hate them. It is no longer an innocent kind of bitterness that can be "outgrown." It is a real hatred that makes mortal enemies of flesh-and-blood relatives.

A New Sex Drug — 2

I believe a new sex drug will be concocted and distributed soon by the black market to teen-agers and students. It will break down moral restraint and lead thousands of teen-agers into promiscuous sex activity. At the same time, I see a tremendous change coming to the entire drug culture. Outside of this sex drug that I predict is coming, this generation will not be lost to drugs.

Marijuana will be legalized. Anything we can't handle, we legalize. But legalized marijuana will lead to boredom. There will be more dissatisfied adults smoking pot than teen-agers looking for a thrill. Pot will be an adult problem in the future.

LSD, speed, and other psychedelics will become less and less popular. I predict that students will be going more toward spiritual highs rather than chemical highs. We will always have a drug problem in this nation, but it will not be nearly as big a problem as hatred in the home.

Teen-age Alcoholism Will Increase — 3

While so much attention is being given to drug abuse, a growing number of teen-agers and students will turn to drink. We are going to face a critical drinking problem with teen-agers between thirteen and sixteen years of age. It is, in part, a backlash from all the teaching in our schools about the dangers of narcotics. We have succeeded in frightening pre-teeners away from hard drugs, but we have not emphasized the dangers of alcohol. Consequently, many kids who were told by their parents that parental drinking habits were not as bad as teen-age narcotic habits have decided to drop drugs and take up alcohol.

However, even though I am predicting a tragic increase in teen-age alcoholism, I am also convinced that it will not be nearly as big a problem as bitterness toward parents. Actually, bitterness toward dad and mom will be the reason why many will turn to drink.

Kids Are Being Provoked — 4

The Bible warns parents against provoking their children to anger, but this commandment is being ignored by a great majority of parents. In the past, when young people felt betrayed and provoked by the establishment and by the government, they took to the streets, demonstrating, rioting, and resisting. Hating politicians and despising government leaders, students vented their anger by attempting to overthrow the system. The revolution has temporarily quieted down, and many former rebels are now trying to work within the system to change it.

But watch out! The anger that led students to riot in the streets is still seething beneath the surface. It is now being directed toward hypocritical parents who preach one thing to their teen-agers while they themselves live something else. I see coming a rising tide of anger among teen-agers especially, and it is going to break out as a new kind of demonstration in the home.

Hatred is going to spread. As parents provoke their children to anger by poor examples and harsh attitudes, this hatred will take deep root and will cause many to forsake home and to run off, hoping to find understanding.

Even ministers of the gospel will not be able to escape this coming problem. Bitterness and rebellion from teen-agers will strike the best of homes in this nation. It will be a hatred and bitterness that will stagger and frighten parents. Many will not understand how to cope with it, and most parents will not even comprehend how and where it started.

One thing is certain. Parents are going to feel betrayed, unwanted, and hated. This hatred and bitterness will be so widespread that I believe it will be the nation's number one problem in the very near future.

Hassle Over Fashions — 5

Changing fashions will continue to be one of the major factors causing this breakdown in communication. Parents, confused by the fast pace of change, will react with firm discipline but without much love or understanding. Hair styles, funky clothes, freaky music, and lazy attitudes about dress will continue to be the major cause of misunderstanding. Teen-agers of the future will not even begin to understand their parents' point of view and will simply "turn them off." This will lead to shipwreck and disaster in many homes.

Overly strict parents are going to be the hardest-hit of all. In an honest effort to maintain old-fashioned standards, some parents are going to find it necessary to exert tremendous pressure on their teen-agers to conform to their ideas of dress and behavior. But the pressures among their own peers will be so strong that it will cause many sincere teen-agers to accept the ideas of their own friends and to reject the rules of their parents.

On the other hand, those parents who become overly permissive and allow their teen-agers to dress and act as they please will soon discover that the teen-agers do not know how to handle so much freedom so early in life. They will go too far too fast and will, at the same time, resent their parents for not providing some kind of discipline. Parents will find it increasingly difficult to know how to deal with changing moods and fashions. It will take supernatural and divine guidance, and only those who are granted wisdom from Heaven will know how to cope with it.

A Reaction Against Spiritual Emptiness — 6

The bitterness and rebellion that I see coming among teen-agers will be caused, in part, by the spiritual emptiness in many homes. Spiritually void parents have lately been discouraging their children from getting involved with "Jesus fanatics." Parents have become more concerned about their social standing than the spiritual condition of their children.

Within this next decade, teen-agers are going to face apocalyptic crises. They are going to be living in a world that is shaken to its very foundation. There will be wars, rumors of wars, and unrest of nations, worldwide. There will be calamities, earthquakes, pestilences, and drastic weather changes that frighten and startle their young minds. Parents who have neglected to provide spiritual guidance and eternal hope are going to face a payday. Teen-agers are going to resent parents who have robbed them of this experience.

The home that has had no God, no church, no spiritual teaching, no Bible, and no hunger for God is headed straight for disaster. I am not preaching now; I am prophesying. I predict that teen-agers raised in such homes are going to turn on their parents with venom, hatred, and rebellion.

A Younger Radical Is Coming — 7

The radicals of the near future will be younger than those of today, better educated, and totally alienated from father and mother. We are about to reap a tragic harvest as a result of recent years of parental neglect, apathy, permissiveness, and over-protectiveness—and an astronomical divorce rate.

Many of these radicals will be pre-teeners who will speak out in their own underground newspapers against the hypocrisy of parents.

The teen gangs of the future in our major cities

will be younger, more vicious, and more down on parents. These "baby gangs," who have been raised on TV crime, TV dinners, and baby sitters, will turn against their parents with a passion. Many of these young children already feel like total strangers to their fathers and mothers. It will be easy for them to hate because they have known so little about real love.

Pay day Is Coming for Divorce — 8

The life and death battle for survival for millions of innocent children will be lost because of divorce. One out of every two and a half marriages now ends in divorce, and pay day is about to come. While divorce has become epidemic, more and more children have become scarred and damaged as a result. The homes of some of the most "ideal" couples are now breaking up, and the children are caught in the middle.

Picture an army of millions of little children, who have been traumatically wounded and scarred by divorce and separation of their parents, now growing up as young teen-agers ready to settle the score. They have been taught to hate one or both of their parents because there was no middle ground left. It is a revolution that has moved off the streets into the homes.

Death to Parents — 9

The Bible clearly predicts that a day will come when sons and daughters will betray their parents and will even cause them to be put to death. I could never understand that prophecy until now. It actually means that we face undeclared war in our homes, with a man's worst enemies being those children of his own household—the father turning against son, mother against daughter, and betrayal of all family ties.

Many parents will "die a thousand deaths" because of the tragic betrayal of their very own children. But these children are going to betray for what they believe is a legitimate reason. Many of these parents have not even tried to stick it out. They've become so involved with their own problems and hang-ups that they have had little or no time to deal with their children about problems that bother them. Kids have been left to handle their own problems and they can't manage them. They have witnessed their parents cheating on one another, lying, fighting, and running off.

Rebellion of Preachers' Kids — 10

Along with those who rise up in rebellion will be the sons and daughters of ministers, who one day will stand before dad or mother and say with hatred:

You are a phony. You've preached one thing and lived another. You said your marriage was impossible to work out, and yet you expected me to handle impossible problems without giving in. Get lost now, old man! And don't do any more preaching to me. You couldn't handle the problems of life, so you have nothing at all to say to me.

The Bible says that godly mothers will live to hear their daughters rise up and call them blessed. But in this next decade, many, many mothers are going to live to see their daughters rise up and curse them. A generation of teen-age girls will rise up and curse a generation of mothers who were caught up in a sensuous world of drinking, carousing, smoking, cheating, and divorcing.

There are some instances when divorce cannot be avoided. But in those instances, God has a way of balancing the books and keeping the home together. Children can survive without bitterness and rebellion and can still love both their parents when an unreconcilable situation has been healed through prayer and the power of God.

Fewer Runaways — 11

In the next decade there will be fewer runaways and more kids staying at home to make it miserable on their parents. Most parents do not want to go to the trouble of reporting their kids as missing and would rather have them home to let them have their own way than to risk the embarrassment of a runaway. Parents in the future are going to make it clear to their teen-agers that they have no need to run away. Many parents are simply going to give up and tell their children, "Take what you want. Do as you please—just don't run away."

The inducements once available only out on the street are now available in many homes. It will be possible to be a runaway at heart and still remain at home. Kids will be able to neglect their parents, live under the same roof, but not even communicate. They will not even be expected to communicate, and little will be expected in the way of understanding or friendship. They will be like enemies living in a war zone under a truce.

Hell for Hypocrites — 12

Parents who smoke, drink, and cheat, while lecturing their kids about morals, will completely lose all influence over their children because of their own hypocrisy. Young people will no longer be in a mood to obey parents who preach one thing and live another. Young people will demand their parents to "show me." Parents who suck cocktails and chain-smoke cigarettes will no longer be able to tell their kids to "quit smoking pot." I see coming, in the not-too-distant future, a total revulsion from all parental hypocrisies by young people.

Preachers who smoke and then stand in the pulpits preaching against drug abuse by teen-agers will be scoffed at for their hypocrisy. Ministers and parents who have excused their hang-ups and habits as being less sinful than the habits and sins of teen-agers are going to have to give an account. The preaching of hypocrites will lose all its influence.

A Supernatural Yearning for Love — 13

While many homes are breaking up, while divorce is on the increase, and while many lives are being shipwrecked, I see developing, nationwide, a hunger among young people for the security of a loving home and family. This yearning will become deeper in the years immediately ahead. While hatred abounds and bitterness grows, there will be a cry for parental love and guidance.

A Counterrevolution of Love — 14

The Bible predicts that when the enemy comes in like a flood, the Spirit of the Lord will raise up a standard against him. In the midst of this revolution of the home, I see a counterrevolution developing. I hear the tearful, heartbroken cry of thousands upon thousands of young people who yearn to live in a home where there is peace, security, and love. And God is going to intervene. There is going to be a supernatural awakening in the middle of this rebellion. The Holy Spirit is going to heal and restore many. He will turn the hearts of many children back to their parents and will bring them together again. This, of course, is only for those who heed the call of the Spirit.

I see the Holy Spirit mending the hearts and minds of children shattered by broken homes. I see hope and miraculous cures in the midst of despair and confusion.

PERSECUTION MADNESS 5

A "Spirit of Persecution" Is Coming — 1

I see an hour of persecution coming such as mankind has never before witnessed. This will be a persecution of true Jesus believers that will soon arise
like a many-headed monster out of the sea. It will
begin slowly and subtly, coming at a time when religious freedom appears to be at a peak. It will
spread throughout the United States, Canada, and
the entire world and will finally become a kind of
madness.

An antichrist spirit will enter the hearts of certain men in high places, in government, and in the
judicial system, causing these officials to engage in
legal maneuvers designed to harass independent
churches, missionaries, and ministers. There is already much evidence that this harassment has now
started. I see a time coming when nearly all evan-

gelical missionary projects, all religious radio and TV programming, and all incorporated missionary societies will be so closely monitored, questioned, and badgered that they will be cautious of expanding in any area.

The Rise of a Super World Church — 2

I see the formation of a super world church consisting of a union between liberal ecumenical Protestants and the Roman Catholic church, joining politically hand in hand, creating one of the most powerful religious forces on earth.

This super world church will be spiritual in name only, freely using the name of Jesus Christ, but will, in fact, be antichrist and political in many of its activities. This powerful church union will be deeply involved in social action, tremendous charity programs, and ministries of compassion. Its leaders will make sweeping statements about meeting human need by sending out a call for renewed social action, political intervention, and a greater voice in world affairs.

A Sudden "Mysterious" Chain of Events — 3

Just when it appears that the ecumenical movement is nearly dead, a rather mysterious chain of events will bring about the framework for this union. Rome will insist upon and receive many concessions from the Protestant ecumenical leaders.

The Pope will be considered more of a political than a spiritual leader of this great union. Protestant leaders of the ecumenical movement will insist upon and receive certain concessions from Rome in exchange. They will not be asked to consider the Holy Father as the infallible head of the church and will accept his political leadership without accepting his role as Peter's successor.

I am in no way suggesting that the Pope or any other church leader involved in this super church organization will be engaging in antichrist activity. The Bible has much to say on that matter but it is not for me, at this time, to speculate on the subject. However, I do see something that frightens me. I see an army of career people invading the most influential posts in this super church organization. Many of them will be ungodly, antichrist people, obsessed with the concept that this super church must become a political power, strong enough to put pressure on all those who oppose its actions. While those in the highest posts of leadership will be speaking about miracles, love, and reconciliation, hirelings who work under them will be harassing and persecuting those religious organizations opposed to their leadership.

The formation of this super world church will begin in a small way. It will start with informal cooperative study and research programs. Other co-operative programs will be initiated without legal or binding commitments from Protestants or Catholics. But liberal Protestant leaders from England and the United States will join liberal Catholic theologians from Europe in pressing for an "ecumenical miracle."

The legal, political amalgamation is yet quite distant—but the informal framework for the union is already under way.

Homosexuals and Lesbians
Welcomed by Super Church — 4

I see this super church, in the guise of "understanding," accepting homosexuals and lesbians into its membership. Homosexual and lesbian love will be vindicated by the leadership of this church union and will not only be welcomed but will be encouraged.

Homosexual and lesbian ministers will be ordained and given places of authority in this church union, and will be heralded as a new breed of pioneer introducing new concepts of love and evangelism.

I see coming, in nearly every major city in the United States and around the world, homosexual and lesbian churches catering exclusively to the spiritual needs of their own kind, with full recognition and support from organized religion. Sunday school and church literature will be distributed in study curriculum suggesting to children and teenagers that homosexuality is a normal and acceptable form of Christian sexual practice.

Most tragic of all, I see the day coming when the majority of homosexuals will no longer seek help from the church. Instead, they will be defended by the super church, and admired for their courage and willingness to be different. This super church will accommodate itself to the weaknesses of man's flesh and will set out to comfort mankind in their sins. Guilt complexes will be blamed on old-fashioned "sin condemning" preachers who speak out against the hang-ups of those who were once considered candidates for help and counseling. New teaching efforts will be focused on an attempt to enlighten men on how to live with their problems and, in fact, to enjoy these weaknesses as "gifts from God."

Nude Dancing in Church — 5

Nude dancing in certain of these member churches will be excused as "artistic forms of worship." Men will become worshippers of the creature more than of the Creator, and God will be forced to give these kinds of worshippers over to their sins. As a result, many will be given over to reprobate minds, creating a new form of mental illness that will not respond to any kind of treatment. Public nudity in any form is creature-worship. Nudity in the church will not go unanswered by God. The Bible clearly states that this form of worship inevitably leads to severe mental problems.

Although nude dancing will not become widespread, it will continue to be accepted by many church leaders as a legitimate expression of worshippers seeking to find "the beauty of soul through the beauty of human form."

Occult Practices Within the Church — 6

I believe the super world church will condone certain occult practices. Already some church groups in Haiti have incorporated certain aspects of voodoo into their form of worship. Study committees will be established to "defang" the devil and remake his image into one of a bland nonentity, not to be feared.

In some of the most respected, wealthy churches in the country, seances will replace prayer meetings. A growing number of ministers will be intrigued by the supernatural claims of spiritualistic and satanist groups. I see the day coming when those ministers who have never been very close with God will become very close to the devil.

Satan will appear as an angel of light to deceive, if it were possible, the elect, the chosen of God. Satan's own ministers will appear as angels of light and they will attempt to spread the message within the ranks of the church that Satan is not an enemy, but a friend.

The super church will never officially accept occult practices outright, but phrenology, palmistry, fortune telling, and horoscopes will be widely respected.

The Rise of a Supernatural Church — 7

I see a great and supernatural union of all the true followers of Jesus Christ, bound together through the Holy Spirit and mutual confidence in Christ and His Word. This supernatural church of Bible believers will become a kind of underground fellowship and will include Catholics and Protestants of all denominations. It will bind together young and old, black and white, and people of all nations.

While the visible super world church gains political power, this invisible supernatural church will grow tremendously in spiritual power. This power will come from persecution. The persecution madness that is coming upon this earth will drive these Christians closer together and closer to Jesus Christ. There will be less concern for denominational concepts and more emphasis on the return of Jesus Christ. The Holy Spirit will bring together, in one, people from all faiths and walks of life.

Although this supernatural church already exists around the world, in days to come it will become politically more and more invisible. But as persecution becomes more intense, this body of believers will become almost radical in its evangelistic efforts. This invisible church will receive supernatural unction and Holy Ghost power to continue preaching the gospel until the ends of the earth have heard.

Special Persecution for Charismatic Catholics — 8

Charismatic Catholics who consider themselves members of the invisible supernatural church of Jesus Christ will face an hour of grievous persecution. The Roman Catholic church is about to "pull in" the welcome mat to all Catholics who speak with tongues and who lean toward Pentecostal teachings concerning the Holy Spirit. High-level political pressure will be placed on priests to "put the fire out."

Watch for the Pope to take a negative stand against the Charismatic movement within the Catholic church. The honeymoon is about over. Catholic magazines will soon begin to speak out against the movement within its ranks and call for a purging. It will begin as a slow trend but will gather momentum quickly, until all Catholics in this movement will eventually face real persecution from within their own church.

The Charismatic movement within the Catholic church will become so powerful and widespread it will appear to some leaders as a threat to those who do not understand what it means. More than 500,000 may be involved in the Charismatic Catholic movement within a short time. Those not in this movement will accuse it of lacking social concern and of being too oblivious to the traditions of the church. They will be accused of turning away from the Virgin Mary and negating the authority of the Pope.

Let every Catholic who boasts about having "the baptism with the Holy Ghost" prepare for persecution. It will not happen overnight, but most assuredly the day is coming when every Catholic who has experienced a "Pentecost" will be forced to determine how meaningful their "baptism" really is. Some will be forced to return to tradition and will allow their experience to lie dormant. Many others, however, will begin to discover that they have more Christian love, fellowship, and spiritual rapport with other Protestants and Catholics who have centered their lives around the person of Jesus Christ and the fullness of the Holy Spirit.

Many will not believe me, but I see a day coming when many Protestants as well as Catholics must "come out from among them." These new Christians will not call themselves Protestant or Catholic but simply "Renewed" Christians. Their fellowship will not be based on the experience of speaking with tongues, but will be centered on the Father and His Son, Jesus Christ.

Persecution of Charismatic Catholics by the hierarchy of the church will not stop the renewal with that church. Instead, the ministry of the Holy Spirit will accomplish great miracles, and the numbers of Catholics joining "renewal" groups will increase under persecution.

Emphasis on "speaking with tongues" will diminish. Instead, there will evolve a "spiritual brotherhood" ministry, based on solid Bible teaching and mutual love and understanding for other true followers of Jesus Christ. It will become a kind of "spiritual priesthood" for laymen who want to help "bear one another's burdens."

Persecution Through a Media Struggle — 9

There is at present tremendous freedom for the preaching of the true gospel on radio and television. Never have the doors been so open to ministers of Christ in all the media. Christians now own and operate their own radio and TV stations, and they are at liberty to pray for the sick, raise money, and promote the gospel in any way they see fit. But watch out! Persecution and harassment are coming. There is a sound of change in the air. Christ-centered radio and TV programming will become the target of satanic forces determined to force them off the airways.

Already, there is a behind-the-scenes movement to establish a kind of rating system for all religious radio and TV programming. Liberal church leaders will attempt to establish a kind of screening board and to force themselves on the FCC as the final authority on all paid and sustaining free time on the media. No program would be aired without their approval. The result would be a bland "Christless" gospel that offended no one.

The doors, now wide open, are slowly but surely going to close. Christian radio and TV stations should begin to expect persecution and harassment. Atheistic and antichrist forces are even now preparing litigation against certain religious stations and evangelists. I see Satan trying to bog down these programs and stations in red tape, legal proceedings, and tax problems. Satan will use every tactic at his disposal to remove all Christ-centered programs from the media.

The message I receive for all those ministries using the media to spread the gospel is this—

Work while it is yet day, for the night cometh when no man can work.

This is the daytime of freedom and opportunity, but the nighttime of harassment and persecution is not far off. When that nighttime of persecution comes, perhaps few, if any, will be effectively ministering through the media.

Persecution From Hollywood — 10

Look for Hollywood to step up its attack against true religion with more exposé-type movies. The film *Marjoe* was the most brazen attempt by satanic forces to put down and ridicule all religion having to do with the blood of Jesus Christ. Revivalists and evangelical ministers will continue to be stereotyped as Elmer Gantrys, charlatans, cheats, and money-mad comedians.

More and more movie makers will attempt to debunk puritanical moral values. Gospel-preaching churches and ministers will come under special attack, while at the same time the occult and witchcraft will be glorified and sensationalized.

I see coming a sophisticated attempt by intellectuals to "preach out" in films against all "revival type" Christians. A kind of atheistic "snobbery" will motivate a new breed of movie makers into an obsession against any and all religion that inhibits man's hedonistic desires.

Persecution From TV Comedies — 11

TV comedy shows will become bolder and bolder in poking fun at Christ and true Christians. Comedy writers will mete out blow after blow through comedy shows designed to put down sacred traditions. Eventually these shows will be punctuated with four-letter words, and anything will go. Television programming will become absolutely blasphemous and millions of unbelievers will be able to sit in front of their TV sets laughing and mocking as subjects once considered sacred are undermined.

I am not suggesting TV comedy writers have joined some kind of conspiracy against God or religion. What I perceive is writers trying to compete with one another to see who can do the best job of "putting down" sacred traditions and teachings. It is a very subtle attack against the teachings of Jesus Christ, camouflaged by comedy. Already, comedy shows poke fun at Kathryn Kuhlman (the famous woman evangelist), Billy Graham, Oral Roberts—and lately, even the Pope. The worst is yet to come. The most anti christ comedy ever devised will be aired on network TV, without opposition!

Persecution Through Taxation of Churches — 12

There is coming an attempt to tax churches and church-related organizations. Atheistic forces, with the help of the American Civil Liberties Union, will push this matter all the way to the Supreme Court. A temporary setback will not stop them from pushing for Congressional action. A legal setback by the courts will not stop their long-range action.

In spite of recent court decisions, we will eventually have taxation of churches. It will begin as an insignificant kind of nuisance tax, but will soon burgeon into a monster-size tax that will push some independent churches and missionary societies near bankruptcy.

Church-related businesses will be taxed first. That will soon be followed by taxation of all church-owned properties, including parsonages. Church buildings will be exempt.

Some very serious court battles lie ahead in regard to this issue, and even Supreme Court decisions can be overturned.

I do not see church budgets or church buildings being taxed in the near future—but I do see taxation of church-related enterprises coming soon. I see a "snowball" effect and the government will one day be so deeply involved in taxation of church properties that an entire catalog of guidelines will be needed.

The IRS may, one day, become one of the most powerful weapons against the church. It would then be possible for government agencies to maintain a stranglehold on churches. Government agencies are soon going to be delving into the private books of almost every nonprofit religious organization. Those who do not comply with stringent guidelines will be forced to shut down—and there will be no recourse.

The Undermining of Christian Education — 13

I see three distinct ways in which Satan will attempt to undermine Christian education. Christian schools, colleges, and universities will not escape the coming hour of persecution and harassment. First, expect political harassment, red tape, and very acute financial problems. Federal and state aid will come with more and more strings attached.

Second, expect an almost unexplainable student mood of apathy, unrest, and disrespect for leadership.

Third, expect the faculty to be infiltrated by teachers and professors who are unwitting tools in the hands of Satan to undermine the foundations of faith and leadership. Satan will attempt to wrest the leadership of these schools and institutions out of the hands of true men of God and place them in the hands of compromising liberals who will not attempt to check the movement toward agnosticism.

Some campuses will experience spiritual awakenings, but they will be short-lived and will not affect the great masses of students.

The leadership of Christian educational institutions must prepare themselves for difficult times ahead—both financially and spiritually. Those who believe in the power of prayer will suffer less. Those who give priority to spiritual matters will experience supernatural intervention and help. For certain, there is trouble ahead on the campus. The financial squeeze will be formidable, and only a miracle will keep some schools open. A few will not survive.

The Jesus Revolution Goes Sour — 14

The Jesus revolution among young people will level off, and undisciplined followers will return to their drugs, their free sex, their old ways of life. Persecution will separate the sheep from the goats. Only totally surrendered disciples will be left standing when the fog clears.

The time is soon coming when it will no longer be popular to be a Jesus person. Jesus songs will not be on hit parades and His name will no longer be a commercial asset to Broadway or Hollywood. The world that once used the name of Jesus so promiscuously is going to turn on Him and put Him down.

I see a replay of the first recorded Jesus movement in history. Jesus came riding into Jerusalem on a donkey to the hurrahs and hosannas of thousands caught up in the excitement of a Jesus movement. Young and old alike ripped branches from palm trees and spread their jackets on the ground so the little donkey could walk over them. They cried, "Jesus, Jesus! Hosanna to the King!" But that first Jesus movement went sour. A very short time later that same Jesus stood before an angry crowd that screamed, "Crucify Him! Away with Him! Imposter!" The crowd turned against Him.

The modern Jesus movement has had its crowds, too. They have sung the praises of Jesus. Jesus has really been in.

A "Hate Christ" Movement — 15

But look what is happening today. Many joy-poppers are going back to their drugs, and a Jesus "revulsion" movement is springing up. Young devil worshippers and occultists are becoming a nucleus of a "hate Christ" type of movement, whose chief aim is to harass Jesus people and refute the claims of Christ. Out of this Jesus movement is coming a hard core of true Jesus people who have completely repudiated their old way of life. They have forsaken their old habits and are committed to a life of service to Jesus Christ.

My message to true Jesus people is loud and clear. Prepare for the coming persecution. Prepare to face these "hate Christ" clubs in school. In many places, Christian young people who take an open stand for Christ will be verbally stoned by those their own age. This revulsion movement against Christ will be personally directed by Satan and carried on by those who are deeply committed to the occult.

Jesus people will not only be considered freaks; they will also be called all manner of names and will even be spat upon in the corridors of high schools and colleges. The day may come when Bibles will be plucked from their arms and ripped apart by a laughing crowd of mockers. The harassment may eventually become so violent and widespread that Christian young people will either harden themselves like steel to withstand it or crumble before it and deny their faith.

Satan Ministers — 16

There will be "Satan evangelists," mostly young people who will actually preach about the power of Satan and who will zealously work at making converts. Ouija boards, tarot cards, horoscopes, and occult books will be passed around and devoured by young people seeking truth.

We are going to pay a price for what we believe. Do not think that Christians can escape the trial that is coming. Your endurance will be tested. It will come upon us so undetected and so subtly that we will not recognize it at first. But when it begins, it will fall upon us with lightninglike strokes. The world will not believe what is happening, because it will fall as a madness upon the earth.

Spiritual Awakening Behind the
Iron and Bamboo Curtains — 17

While free nations experience a wave of real persecution, the Iron and Bamboo Curtain countries will experience a short period of spiritual awakening. Those who have lived under terrible religious persecution will enjoy a limited period of freedom. God's Holy Spirit will split the Iron and Bamboo Curtains and will seek out and find hungry hearts in Russia, China, and Eastern Europe.

God has promised to pour His Spirit out upon all flesh, and that includes the peoples behind the Iron and Bamboo Curtains.

God is bringing to pass a temporary truce between the East and the West for the express purpose of getting the gospel into these Communist countries. Japanese and Korean Christians alone can be used of God to reach thousands in China. Christians in West Germany can reach those in East Germany. The path to Russia is through Finland. A tremendous move of the Holy Spirit in Finland can and will spill over into Russia.

Ironically, while the doors are beginning to close on this side of the Curtains, the doors will begin to open on the other side. And, after a short period of freedom and spiritual awakening among many, the doors will suddenly close, and the persecution madness will begin with intensity and engulf all those nations.

GOD'S MESSAGE TO THE UNPREPARED 6

We are about to move out of the age of Aquarius into an age the Bible describes as "the day of sorrows." Jesus himself warned about a "great tribulation" coming upon the earth such as never before witnessed in history.

The Predictions of Jesus — 1

Don't let anyone fool you. For many will come claiming to be the Messiah, but will lead many astray. You will hear of wars. The nations and kingdoms will rise against each other. There will be famines and earthquakes in many places. BUT ALL OF THIS WILL BE ONLY THE

BEGINNING OF HORRORS TO
COME! Sin will be rampant everywhere.
The Good News will be preached through-
out the world and then shall the end
come. (Matthew 24:4-8,12,14 Living New
Testament)

Tribulation Is Coming — 2

A dictionary defines "tribulation" as *distress, af-
fliction, and suffering*—and this great tribulation is
to be a time of unbelievable suffering and crises.
God, by His Holy Spirit, is calling mankind to prepare for the end of all things. He is allowing nature
to pound this earth with one crisis after another to
warn of the approaching day of wrath and judgment.

Can we believe the predictions of Jesus? In an
age of increased knowledge, of great scientific
achievement, can we really accept the idea of a
world in complete chaos?

Are the Bible prophecies to be taken literally?
Will there be a final world war involving every nation, as described in God's Word? Will there be
even worse famines, plagues, earthquakes, floods,
and other severe weather changes—as clearly described in the Bible?

War and Terrorism — 3

Will we see war, acts of terrorism, and violence all around? Will there be a collapse of all moral standards and laws—as well as a worldwide depression with runaway inflation and devastated economy?

Is there really going to be a short period of fragile peace on earth when men everywhere are yearning and crying for a return to tranquility? And will that time of fragile peace precede the impending doom predicted in the Bible?

Can we really believe the Bible when it states that men will one day say, "We will outlive all these crises. We will have peace and prosperity." Then suddenly the world will be drawn into a final destructive world war. Is there really an Armageddon coming?

Over Two Billion Killed — 4

The human mind is boggled by Bible prophecies if they are taken literally. If we believe the literal interpretation of the Bible, there is coming a final world war and tribulation in which over two billion people will be killed. Death will come from war, famines, plagues, earthquakes, floods, and severe weather changes worldwide.

The Bible clearly predicts that men will scoff at

such prophecies and predictions as those being made in this vision.

Noah's Prediction Ignored — 5

People in Noah's day didn't believe a flood of judgment was coming to the earth, and they spent their time in revelry, laughing at the crazy prophet who was preaching a vision. The Bible says, "They knew not until the flood came and took them all away." Jesus said men and women will likewise continue in sex sin, rebellion, violence, and immorality until the end of time. They will not accept visions or predictions of impending doom or judgment.

Yet, with all the scoffing and ridicule this kind of message receives from intellectuals and church leaders, the great majority of young people today are concerned with apocalyptic prophecies. Nowadays it is not only Christians who are expecting an end of the world as predicted in the Bible. Even *Time* magazine recently did a serious treatment of the subject. There are now many thinking scientists and intellectuals, behaviorists and technicians who also warn that world history could likely come to a cataclysmic end in the near future.

The message of this vision will be called a fanatical attempt to scare the unconverted. Others will fault it because of all the "wrath and judgment." Men choose so often to see only the one side of God —His love and mercy. But God has another side to

His personality. Even a surface check of God's Word will easily prove it. Paul the apostle said:

> Knowing the terror of the Lord we persuade men. (II Corinthians 5:11)

A World Out Of Control — 6

If you think my vision is scary or "too far out"—let me give you a clear chronology of what the Bible predicts is coming.

The Bible clearly predicts that the world will apparently go "out of control," that cities will become unmanageable, and that countries will be ungovernable. People will begin to reject God completely. Mankind will become greedy and materialistic. There will be trouble-making rebels taking over institutions, and people in the midst of this crisis will be "enjoying themselves in every evil way imaginable."

Thousands of Christians will fall away and begin to betray their friends. They will be hotheaded, puffed up with pride, and will prefer "good times" to worshipping God. They will become lovers of pleasure more than lovers of God. Normal times will disappear, and there will appear the addict, the prostitute, the homosexual, the thief, and the street-gang killer.

In spite of an "increase in knowledge," human nature will become a slave to immorality, violence, and rebellion.

The Bible predicts a day of total terrorism and

violence. Immorality of unbelievable dimensions will surround Christians and vex their souls almost to death. Satan will attempt to discredit and destroy the work of the Holy Spirit.

Whole nations will follow philosophies of godless rebellion and false religious cults.

The world is going to maneuver itself into a position of lawlessness and recklessness, that can be brought together only by a super dictator who lays claim to supernatural powers.

Israel to Become Invincible — 7

The Bible predicts that in the "last days" the nation of Israel would be reborn. After nearly two thousand years, the Jews who have wandered over the face of the earth oppressed, persecuted, and killed by the enemies of God will return to Palestine and retake their homeland.

In specific fulfillment of Bible prophecy, the nation of Israel was born in May 1948, and began to "bloom as a rose in the desert"—just as the Bible predicted.

The Bible also predicts that a host of enemies would arise against Israel and attempt to plunder the land, but that all enemies would run in defeat with their hearts melting within them. The Bible suggests that one Jew will put to flight more than one thousand enemies. And ten would put ten thousand to flight.

Israel is invincible because it is flowing in the tide of divine prophecy. There is no nation on earth powerful enough to destroy Israel, and only in God's appointed time will an enemy trample through the streets of Jerusalem.

A "United States of the World" — 8

The Bible predicted the birth of the European Common Market. The European Economic Community began its confederacy of six nations after the signing of the Treaty of Rome in 1957. When that treaty was signed, many Bible teachers wondered if this was the fulfillment of the prophecy in the Bible of the resurrection of the ancient Roman Empire. That prophecy stated that ten nations would spring up in the "end times" and would provide a power base for an antichrist. Since the treaty in 1957, four other nations have been added, creating a total of ten. There is continuing talk now about enlarging the community into a "United States of Europe."

The "United States of the World" is just a world depression away. A collapse of the world monetary system could lead to world government headed by a global dictator. The premier of Belgium recently said:

> The method of international committees has failed. What we need is a person of the highest order of experience, of great authority, of wide influence, of great energy—either a civilian or a military man, no matter what his nationality, who will cut all the red tape, shove all the com-

mittees out of the way, wake up all the
people and galvanize all the governments
into action. Let him come quickly. (Quot-
ed in *Le Soir*)

World anarchy and confusion can ripen this
world for an antichrist dictator who will come in
the name of peace to end the desperation and lawlessness that will abound.

A Superstar Antichrist — 9

When you sort out the mystery and the "spook-
iness" of the revelations of God's prophets, you
see clearly a prediction of a coming "superstar Antichrist" who will arise in the last days, defy God,
and persecute true believers. He will come in the
name of peace, law, and order and will succeed in
changing the systems of laws and justice. He will be
exposed as a fraudulent son of Satan.

The Bible predicts that his rule of terror will be
short-lived but totally devastating. This phony dictator who poses as an angel of light will deceive the
whole world.

Think of the powers now claimed by the President of the United States. Men in high places are
grabbing for unprecedented powers. In light of recent developments, it is not very difficult to understand Bible predictions that this Antichrist will sit
as a god on a throne, demanding the worship and
respect of people everywhere.

A Final World War — 10

We are told specifically in the Bible that in the last days the Antichrist and nations will meet in a final war in Israel. It will be the war of all wars.

This war will, no doubt, be caused by a worldwide energy crisis. That's right, a war over oil and energy. Perhaps also over the chemicals in the Dead Sea. These chemicals make explosives. And, because of worldwide famine, the chemicals are needed for fertilizer. The value of these chemicals is estimated to be one trillion dollars. How many of the world's wars have been fought for less?

During World War II, from 1939 to 1944, more than 54 million people were destroyed and millions of others were hurt and maimed by the destruction. In the 1970s, we have had Vietnam, Biafra, and Bangladesh. Our generation has known the horror of more than 65 million dead and 100 million casualties.

But the Bible predicts a final world war at Armageddon that defies comprehension. The Bible talks about the heavens being on fire and the very elements melting with fervent heat.

Specifically the Bible says:

> The day of the Lord is surely coming, as unexpectedly as a thief, and then the heavens will pass away with a terrible noise and the heavenly bodies will disappear in fire, and the earth and everything on it will be burned up. (II Peter 3:10, *The Living Bible*)

The weapons of today, as we all know, are certainly capable of the kind of destruction the Bible describes—such as the holocaust from the heavens destroying one-third of all vegetation.

Israel and surrounding nations have already become arsenals of weapons—stockpiles of napalm, guns, bombs, missiles, and even biological weapons. Mankind now has stockpiled the destructive force to kill every living thing on the face of the planet.

The Bible predicts that during this great tribulation time of judgment, satanic forces with an army of 200 million will kill one-third of the world's population. Today that would mean that about two billion people will be killed. The horror of this cannot be imagined. Thus far our worst world war (World War II) claimed 54 million dead. This last war will kill thirty-seven times as many. It is so gruesome that it is difficult to even think about it.

Increased Devil Worship — 11

The Bible foretells that in spite of the world's tottering on the brink of war and devastation, mankind will turn to the worship of devils, satanic spirits, and idols made from metal, stone, and wood. The increase of occult practices we are now witnessing is clearly predicted in the Bible as a sign of the end times.

Young people today are pledging allegiance to Satan, or they are worshipping the gods of technology and science.

Only a world possessed by demons will be able to

put aside the terror and horror of one-third of mankind killed through war and to fall back into rebellion and immorality.

Strange and Unusual Events — 12

The Bible predicts that unusual and strange signs will appear in the heavens and on the earth beneath. The prophets of the Old Testament called them "woes"—events causing pain and suffering. This describes the terrible famines and plagues in store for us—almost immediately ahead. Famine has already become the world's greatest killer. In Biafra and Bangladesh it has brought suffering and death to untold thousands.

In India the population explodes and the crops fail, while thousands die every day from hunger.

Millions around the world now live in the cesspool surroundings of slums—without food, water, or decent shelter. Millions now grasp at hope, trying to keep themselves alive just one more day. Even in our "civilized" or "developed" nations, the plagues are becoming very real.

Killer Diseases, Rats, Bees — 13

Jesus said that in these days of tribulation, "Men's hearts will fail them for fear of watching what is happening upon the earth." In America, the number one killer disease is already heart failure.

Medical authorities say venereal disease is no

longer just an epidemic—it is an uncontrollable pandemic of frightening proportions.

Scientists warn of new strains of germs, viruses, and vermin that are resistant to poisons and chemicals and threaten to upset the balance of nature.

"Super rats" immune to poisons now infest grain supplies and pass along dreaded diseases to humans.

So-called "killer bees" have been bred in South America and threaten to invade this country. The sting is nearly always fatal.

Unusual weather with rainy, wet summers has caused plagues of mosquitoes. In some areas they have been bad enough to cause cattle to stampede and to cause disease in other life.

In Texas and parts of New Mexico, thousands of cattle have frozen to death. These dead cattle were piled high, soaked with kerosene, and burned. In Africa millions of cattle have died because of a lack of rain and famine conditions. These will become ever-increasing problems.

Food Shortages — 14

Another evidence of the threat of famine is the increase in world population and the decrease in the world's resources and food supplies. Crop failures, plagues of vermin, and diseases will cause terror around the world in the not-too-distant future.

Severe food and energy shortages are predicted in the Bible, and the crisis exists already in many parts of the world. As the world population outstrips food production, the situation will get worse. No improvement is even in sight.

Seven Final Judgments — 15

The Bible describes in the book of Revelation the seven terrible, final plagues to come on the earth—the plagues that are worse than all the others combined.

1. Malignant sores and skin cancers

> And the first went, and poured out his vial upon the earth; and there fell a noisome and grievous sore upon the men which had the mark of the beast, and upon them which worshipped his image. (Revelation 16:2)

The first plague is malignant sores or skin cancer, which afflicts all who have been identified with the government of the Antichrist. The Bible does not tell specifically what causes the malignant sores, but we might assume that a principle we see throughout Scripture will have something to do with it. The Bible says we reap what we sow. We have been sowing sensuality, nudity, and sexual permissiveness. Since venereal disease is now a major problem, this could be a plague of stubborn sores—a contagious new strain of venereal disease.

Another explanation may be a warning offered recently by scientists testifying about effects on the atmosphere by the SST (supersonic transport plane). The SST is now being flown by other nations but is banned from flying over America. Some critics are opposed to the noise pollution of its sonic boom. Others are afraid of what it might do to the atmosphere. Scientists testified that if the SST caused only a 5 percent change in the ozone level of the earth, we are in danger. If that happens, say the scientists, higher levels of deadly radiation will reach us from the sun. When that happens, they predict a massive increase of skin cancer and other malignant sores. More than a 5 percent change could make this outbreak of skin cancer almost universal.

2. *Pollution of the seas*

And the second angel poured out his vial
upon the sea; and it became as the blood
of a dead man: and every living soul died
in the sea. (Revelation 16:3)

The second final judgment is pollution of the ocean. The Bible predicts that it will become as the "blood of a dead man." The Bible clearly predicts the death of living creatures in the sea.

3. *Pollution of rivers and inland waters*

And the third angel poured out his vial
upon the rivers and fountains of waters;
and they became blood. (Revelation 16:4)

The third judgment is the pollution of rivers and the fountains of waters. Man's present interest in the pollution of our environment is not accidental. Mankind is now playing out a part clearly predicted in the book of Revelation. There is to be a poisoning of the fresh water supplies of the earth. When the Bible describes our water supply as becoming as the "blood of a dead man," it is describing the death and corruption we have already witnessed in our generation. It is to get worse.

4. *Killer heat waves—sun scorching*

> And the fourth angel poured out his vial upon the sun; and power was given unto him to scorch men with fire. And men were scorched with great heat, and blasphemed the name of God, which hath power over these plagues: and they repented not to give him glory. (Revelation 16:8,9)

During this time the Bible also predicts that the sun will be scorching men with fire. It may be that God will send out solar flares of great intensity that will scorch the earth. Or it may be that man's technology will upset the balance of nature, which, in turn, causes severe weather changes, such as record heat waves. In India in May 1972, more than five hundred people died from heat stroke. Are similar, more intense heat waves in store? Add this to the more intense ultraviolet radiation from solar flares and the energy crises that render air conditioning useless—and you have the picture of the horror to come.

This intense scorching of the earth can cause tremendous forest fires across the earth. In California alone, man has upset the balance of nature by introducing a eucalyptus tree which has no apparent use. There are millions of these trees which are now full grown, and scientists estimate that 90 percent of them are dead—the result of a record-breaking freeze in 1972. Severe heat waves could cause these trees to literally explode in fire. The oily bark hanging high in the trees is a tender, dry kindling that turns a burning tree into a giant torch. And, if this burning occurs worldwide and the debris goes into the atmosphere with smoke, it will also likely affect the weather by the darkening of the sun.

Imagine a nightmare world where the sun is scorching the earth, overworking power plants and air conditioning, and triggering massive power blackouts.

5. *International blackouts*

And the fifth angel poured out his vial upon the seat of the beast; and his kingdom was full of darkness; and they gnawed their tongues for pain. (Revelation 16:10)

The fifth judgment is described as a time "full of darkness," causing men to gnaw their tongues for pain and blaspheme the God of Heaven. Millions of people in New York City, London, and other major cities understand what a blackout means. The Bible predicts that the whole world is going to face an unbelievable kind of blackout. Something is to happen that will cause the light of the sun, moon, and stars to be dimmed.

This may be another instance of supernatural darkness, such as that in the plagues in Egypt and the darkness during the Crucifixion. Or it may refer to severe power blackouts from fuel shortages, which could eliminate up to eight hours or one-third of our daily light. Or it may refer to severe weather or atmospheric changes brought on by pollution, natural disasters, or the effects of some of the other judgments. For example, 1816 was called "the year with no summer" because there was frost every single month of the year in parts of northeast America. A foot of snow fell in June. Crop losses were severe. This was caused by tons of volcanic debris from the eruption of the volcano on Tamboro. In 1915, the sun was obscured and the climate was affected.

Is it possible that the industrial pollutants of today could bring this vision to pass? And what about the increasing volcanic activity such as the recent Icelandic eruption? How many volcanic eruptions would it take to blacken the sun?

6. *A bloodbath on Israeli soil*

> And the sixth angel poured out his vial upon the great river Euphrates; and the water thereof was dried up, that the way of the kings of the east might be prepared.
> (Revelation 16:12)

The sixth judgment describes how the blood will flow in Armageddon. This planet's last and most devastating battle will cause death and destruction so complete that the blood from dead armies will flow bridle-deep in an area two hundred miles long. Although soldiers on horseback may seem strangely archaic in this age of tanks and jeeps, we can still assume a literal cavalry force (Rev. 9:15-16, *The Living Bible*), similar to those shown in recent films released by Chinese Communists. Israel, the Arab nations, and the Soviet Union also have large horse cavalry units (Rev. 14:18-20 *The Living Bible*), which may be employed during the battle of Armageddon. One thing is certain. The Bible predicts a bloodbath at Armageddon.

7. Hundred-pound hailstones and earth-shattering quakes

> And the seventh angel poured out his vial into the air; and there came a great voice out of the temple of heaven, from the throne, saying, It is done. And there were voices, and thunders, and lightnings; and there was a great earthquake, such as was not since men were upon the earth, so mighty an earthquake, and so great. (Revelation 16:17,18)

The seventh and final judgment is an earthquake of incredible proportions, accompanied by hailstones weighing up to one hundred pounds each. This earthquake will cause cities to crumble, islands to vanish, and mountains to be flattened.

Some believe that the Bible's description of hundred-pound hailstones really describes a meteorite shower.

In order to grasp the full scope of this terrible wrath and tribulation, just imagine:

> Hitler's ovens
> Stalin's purges
> Biafra
> Nicaragua
> Pakistan
> Bangladesh
> Vietnam

And a whole nightmare of other terrors. Then multiply that horror a thousand times and pack it into a space of just a few years. That will suggest something of what is just ahead in the great tribulation for those who continue to reject God. But that is not all.

Christ Is Coming to Set Up His Kingdom — 16

The most frightening event for the sinner is yet to come. Far and beyond all the horrors, woes, and tribulations described in the Bible is that frightening moment when the sinner must fall on his knees and face Jesus Christ when He comes back to this earth to set up His kingdom. The Bible predicts that the sinner will try to hide in the rocks and crannies and crevices of the mountains. He will cry for the rocks and mountains to fall on him to hide him from the face of Him who sits on the throne.

The Bible predicts the coming of a new heaven and a new earth—renewed by the Holy Spirit. Christ is going to rule as Supreme King and He will do away with wars, disease, disaster, and all that is evil. You can laugh at it, ignore it, and put it aside as a fantastic hoax, but just as surely as the Jew now has returned to his homeland, the Christian is going to sit as the friend of Christ in His coming kingdom. Not one Bible prediction of the past has failed and not one of these future prophecies will fail either. Yes—it is a sordid, sad, frightening, almost unbelievable story of wrath and judgment. But there is absolutely no way to sugarcoat it or ignore it. If you have been rejecting God and refusing His call, I predict that the day will come when you will literally shake in your boots as you see these things come to pass one by one. Survive an earthquake—then see if you can laugh. Watch the latest news developments unfold—then tell me I am a fanatic.

I have seen a vision of coming judgment and the Bible backs it up. The message from God to all the unprepared is loud and clear:

> Wake up! What is happening to the world now is supernatural and there is no turning back. Unless you are on the Lord's side, you cannot survive. There is nothing but fear and despair for those who live selfishly without God.

GOD'S MESSAGE FOR THE PREPARED 7

This has been a good year for bad news. Our daily papers read more like chilling fiction than truth. We get daily doses of news about high food prices, disastrous weather, energy crises, and record-setting storms and floods ravaging the world.

Words like "violent," "record," "unseasonal," and "record-breaking" keep appearing in weather forecasts everywhere. When weather should have been fair and sunny, tornadoes and floods have struck instead. Where weather was once cold, it has become extremely and unseasonally hot.

Meteorologists do their best to predict these disasters and analyze them as they happen, but none of them can explain what is causing disastrous weather changes to happen so frequently.

Many people today are convinced that the world

is out of control. Institutions we have always trusted seem to be falling apart. The government can no longer provide solutions, and even the most astute world leaders are baffled by world conditions. It is shattering to our confidence when high officials shrug their shoulders and confess they understand no more than we do about what is happening. There are no more simple answers to our complex questions.

In light of what we have seen in the last five years in the way of violence, immorality, crime, lawlessness, and tragedy—can you imagine what we are about to witness in the next decade?

The way tragedies and disasters are striking the earth with such frequency and intensity would suggest that the earth is suffering labor pains. The Bible says God is going to create a new heaven and a new earth. This old earth will pass away and melt with fervent heat. The very elements are to be melted away. We are witnessing not so much the death of an old world—but the birth of a new one.

These are exciting days for true Christians. God, in His love and mercy, is allowing disasters to strike the earth to warn all who will hear that Jesus is coming back, and that it's time to get ready. He loves His children too much to bring His new kingdom to pass without warning. He knows that mankind is hard of hearing and that it takes disasters of earthquake proportions to get his attention. These disasters are a kind of countdown, too painful to ignore, choreographed by God to set the stage for the final moments of time. These labor pains will become more frequent and intense as we approach the last hour. There will be more famines, more pestilences, more earthquakes in more places. And all of this is just the beginning of sorrows. Yet the message of the Bible to all true believers is:

> And when these things begin to come to pass, then look up, and lift up your heads; for your redemption draweth nigh. (Luke 21:28)

Men's hearts are failing them from fear over the things happening to this earth. People are hoarding up, saving up, and getting ready for the coming worldwide recession. Even devout Christians are getting caught up in this wave of fear and anxiety about the future. People are afraid the ship is sinking. Mankind is yearning for security, and it has led to an epidemic of "grabbing" for houses, land, money, and guaranteed income.

Does it all sound scary? Is the truth frightening? Is it really possible that the end of the world is really upon us? Is this the very point in time that all the prophets in the Bible predicted would come? Are we actually living in the generation in which all these predictions will be fulfilled? Can even the most devout Christian remotely understand how terribly close this earth is to its midnight hour? One thing is certain—everything appears to be falling apart, as far as the natural eye can discern. Even the most doubtful person on earth must, in his honest moments, admit that something apocalyptic is taking place in the world.

Along with the vision of calamities, God gave me a very special message of hope for all true believers.

I desperately questioned God about all the things I saw coming. I asked Him to show me how Christians could do all they have to do in a limited time when so many were forsaking and going into hiding. How can Christians keep fear out of their hearts? How can they face all the news reports and anticipate all the calamities and disasters without being afraid for their homes and children? Do they abdicate and turn this old world over to the devil and let him have his way? Do they pay off all their bills, salt away some reserves in the bank, then just try to ride it all out—hoping that a better day will come? Do they buy a farm or a piece of land and flee to the country—hoping they can escape the coming tragedies? Will they eat, drink, and be merry—just living it up, knowing they have death hanging over their heads? Do they let their motivation die and surrender to fear? Do they abandon all their dreams and ambitions and become as hermits looking for truth?

Dear friend, hear what the Holy Spirit spoke to me. Just five little words, but so powerful that they awakened in me a glorious new hope and faith. Those five little words are: *God has everything under control!*

That is right—everything is under control. In spite of earthquakes, famines, pestilences, hailstorms, killer heat waves, floods, hurricanes, and epidemics—nature is not out of control! Everything that we see now happening has been clearly predicted in God's Word. Nothing can happen in nature or to nature unless our God allows it. The

Bible predicts that the wrath of God is to be out-poured on this earth through an unleashed nature, designed to warn mankind of the coming judgment.

Nature is controlled and limited by God and it cannot cross those limits unless God permits it. God told Job it was He who:

> Shut up the sea with doors; set bars and doors to stay the proud waves. Took hold of the ends of the earth, that the wicked might be shaken out of it. Reserved the treasures of hail and snow against the day of battle. Divided water courses for the overflow of water. Set the domain of the earth and the ordinances of the heavens. Stayed the bottles of heaven. Sent forth lightnings. And scattered the wind upon the earth. (Job 38)

Child of God, you need no longer fear the un-leashed violence of nature. God is still king of the flood. He is calling, chastising, and warning all His children to heed the signs. But there is a hiding place for believers. The Bible states:

> The angel of the Lord encampeth round about them that fear him, and delivereth them. (Psalms 34:7)

If you trust God, you can look every disaster in the face and proclaim with confidence, "My God is speaking to this universe and His power is being demonstrated. I will just stand still and see the sal-vation of the Lord."

Even Satan is under control. As with Job, God may permit him to touch every material and physi-cal thing around you, but he cannot possess you or rob you of your faith in God. The devil's power is limited and even baby Christians can put Him to flight simply by resisting him through the Word and the blood of Christ. The Bible says, "Resist the devil and he will run from you." Does that sound like defeat? Does that suggest a victorious devil? Does that suggest Christians should fear demon possession? Never!

God has everything under control, and we are under His control. Do not ever fear Satan. It is the fear of the Lord that is the beginning of wisdom. Wherever you got your spirit of fear, you did not get it from God, so why put up with it? Shake it off, because God's message for this hour is:

> God hath not given us the spirit of fear;
> but of power, and of love, and of a sound
> mind. (II Timothy 1:7)

Satan can attempt to swamp you with filth and smut and vex your soul with every imaginable kind of evil. He can persecute you, and the enemies of Christ can revile and hate you. You can wind up penniless, having to pray for your very next meal. You can be hated and rejected by your own family and given up by your closest friends. But the eyes of the Lord are upon the righteous and His ear is open to their prayer. We are not to fear anyone who can destroy the body, but to respect and honor only Him that can touch the soul. No power in heaven or on earth can touch a man's confidence and faith in Jesus Christ. No demon, no devil, no human power can destroy the soul.

You and I, and everything that touches us, are under His control. It's true! No matter how things look in this drunken world, all things are still working together for good to everyone who loves God and are the called according to His purpose.

Let the dollar fail. Let depression or recession come with its unemployment and fear. Let pollution and inflation come. Let there be wars and rumors of wars. Let the fabric of society disintegrate. Let mankind go to the drunken brink of disaster. For the true child of God, everything is still under control! It really doesn't matter—nothing can harm those who abide under the shelter of His almighty wings. The shadow of the Almighty is bigger than any fearful shadow this age can project. God's children need fear no evil. His children will never beg for bread, and He will supply every true need up to the very last minute of time.

God has not promised to keep His children from suffering. He has not promised to keep us from facing an hour of need. We have no promise of world peace, tranquility, security, or continuous financial well-being. We are promised peace and security of soul and mind—the supernatural provision for every true need—and assurance that we would never have to beg for bread. God would rather we all come to the place Paul the apostle came to when he said,

> Having food and raiment let us be there-
> with content. (I Timothy 6:8)

The future looks evil and foreboding. But David said in the Psalms, "I will fear no evil." This is the message for believers today. The future is also under His control, so we need not fear. God has it all preprogrammed. He knows the exact moment

Christ will return. The final tribulation, the judgment, and the battle of Armageddon are all on His calendar. The God who controls all of heaven and earth said:

> The nations are as a drop of a bucket, and are counted as the small dust of the balance: . . . All nations before him are as nothing; . . . less than nothing. (Isaiah 40:15,17)

God wants us to keep working until the return of Christ. That means simply that we are to work as though the end will never come, and live as though it were coming tomorrow.

The great evangelist D. L. Moody was asked, "What would you do today if you knew Jesus Christ was coming tomorrow?" His answer came, "I would plant a tree." So let it be. Let the true Christian go about planting and sowing God's seed and keeping busy doing God's work. When He returns, let Him find us "doing His will."

God is still counting the very hairs on our heads. He is still counting the sparrows that fall. He is still hearing petitions before they are asked. He is still answering before being called. He is still giving abundantly more than we can ask or think. So why be afraid?

I believe the prepared Christian is going to face a time of sorrow and tribulation. I believe he will be tested, tried, and tempted. I believe true Christians are going to witness many of the horrors described in this vision. But I am also firmly convinced in my own heart and mind—and I have the witness of the Holy Spirit in my heart—that God is suddenly

going to deliver His true children from His final
fury that will be outpoured on the earth. He will
deliver His children from the most gruesome hour
of disaster that the Bible predicts will fall upon the
earth.

Prepared Christians—wake up! Everything is
under control and God is at work. He is saving,
healing, baptising, and getting His house in order.
To fear is to blaspheme. We are commanded to en-
courage ourselves in the Lord and to begin to sing
and rejoice as we see the final hour approach. Do I
hear someone ask, "But how can I rejoice when I
see this old sin-cursed world falling apart?" My answer is the Bible answer:

> For we know that the whole creation
> groaneth and travaileth in pain . . . wait-
> ing the redemption. (Romans 8:22,23)

A woman in labor may scream because of pain,
yet in her heart she rejoices because of the fact of
new birth.

The kingdom of God is coming. The kingdom of
Satan is falling. So the Christian can, with confidence, say:

"God has everything under control!"

IT'S YOUR MOVE NOW 8

Job said:

Then Thou scarest me with dreams, and terrifiest me through visions. (Job 7:14)

And this troubled man went on to admit:

I have sinned ... I am a burden to myself. (Job 7:20)

This vision may have turned you off completely. It may have evoked in you disgust, incredulity, or amusement. On the other hand, it may have awakened in you an innate knowledge that it's time to become honest about eternity.

You are not far from God if you have an honest heart. If that is all you can bring to Him, He will accept it. You may have no desire to forsake your present way of life; you may even love your sins and habits. You may honestly not be afraid of the future. You may even be partially content the way you are. But if, in your moment of honesty, you sense an inner nagging about the future, you must do something about it. If you can honestly say to yourself, "I know my life is not what it should be; I know I cannot change myself, so I will ask God to overrule me and help me," then that is a good starting place.

Be absolutely honest. It's time to quit playing games. It's time to quit hiding behind some pet doctrine or theory. It's time to quit excusing yourself through some philosophical escape. It's time to admit that what you know deep in your heart is really true. Something in you is reaching out to God. Something in you cries out for reality, truth, and a solid ground on which to stand.

God states in His Word:

> And ye shall seek me, and find me, when
> ye shall search for me with all your heart.
> (Jeremiah 29:13)

Jesus Christ wants you just as you are—but He wants you to come to Him with an honest heart. If you are ready to quit being a phony, He is ready to meet your honest heart and change your whole lifestyle. Get off your high horse and humble yourself, and a miracle will happen. By faith, you can be born into the coming kingdom of God.

Here is a pattern of an honest prayer. Why not use it, make it personal, and begin here and now.

> Dear Christ Jesus, In all honesty I don't
> know how much I really want to change,
> but I know I must. I can't do it myself, so
> I turn to You for a miracle. Hear my

heart's cry, and look beyond my faults to my need. Forgive and heal me. I confess I do not live up to Your commandments, nor do I truly follow Your Word. But take me as I am and do what You will with me. I open the door and invite You in. Amen.

APPENDIX

APPENDIX I

PREDICTIONS AND PROPHECIES OF BIBLE MEN

Predictions of the Apostle Paul — 1

In the last days it is going to be very difficult to be a Christian. For people will love only themselves and their money; they will be proud and boastful, sneering at God, disobedient to their parents, ungrateful to them and thoroughly bad. They will be hardheaded and never give in to others; they will be constant liars and troublemakers and will think nothing of immorality. They will be rough and cruel, and sneer at those who try to be good. They will betray their friends; they will be hotheaded, puffed up with pride, and prefer good times to worshiping God. They will go to church, yes, but they won't really believe anything they hear. (II Timothy 3:1-5, *The Living Bible*)

The Predictions of Peter — 2

I want to remind you that in the last days there will come scoffers who will do every wrong they can think of, and laugh at the truth. This will be their line of argument: "So Jesus promised to come back, did He? Then where is He? He'll never come! Why, as far back as anyone can remember everything has remained exactly as it was since the first day of creation." (II Peter 3:3-4, *The Living Bible*)

But don't forget this, dear friends, that a day or a thousand years from now is like tomorrow to the Lord. He isn't really being slow about His promised return. . . . But He is waiting, for the good reason that He is not willing that any should perish, and He is giving more time for sinners to repent. The day of the Lord is surely coming, as unexpectedly as a thief, and then the heavens will pass away with a terrible noise and the heavenly bodies will disappear in fire, and the earth and everything on it will be burned up. (II Peter 3:8-10, *The Living Bible*)

God will set the heavens on fire, and the heavenly bodies will melt and disappear in flames. But we are looking forward to God's promise of new heavens and a new earth afterwards, where there will be only goodness. (II Peter 3:12-13, *The Living Bible*)

Predictions of Jude — 3

Dear friends, remember what the apostles of our Lord Jesus Christ told you, that in the last times there would come these scoffers whose whole purpose in life is to enjoy themselves in every evil way imaginable. (Jude 1:17-18, *The Living Bible*)

Predictions of Solomon — 4

"I have called you so often but still you won't come. I have pleaded, but all in vain. For you have spurned my counsel and reproof. Some day you'll be in trouble, and I'll laugh! Mock me, will you?— I'll mock you! When a storm of terror surrounds you, and when you are engulfed by anguish and distress, then I will not answer your cry for help. It will be too late though you search for me ever so anxiously.

"For you closed your eyes to the facts and did not choose to reverence and trust the Lord, and you turned your back on me, spurning my advice. That is why you must eat the bitter fruit of having your own way, and experience the full terrors of the pathway you have chosen. For you turned away from me—to death; your own complacency will kill you. Fools! But all who listen to me shall live in peace and safety, unafraid . . ." (Proverbs 1:24-33, *The Living Bible*)

APPENDIX II

SCRIPTURES TO STUDY

Scriptures for Chapter One

1. "Boast not thyself of to morrow; for thou knowest not what a day may bring forth." (Proverbs 27:1)
2. "Be thou diligent to know the state of thy flocks, and look well to thy herds. For riches are not for ever: and doth the crown endure to every generation?" (Proverbs 27:23,24)
3. "Surely every man walketh in a vain shew: surely they are disquieted in vain: he heapeth up riches, and knoweth not who shall gather them." (Psalms 39:6)
4. "The righteous also shall see, and fear, and shall laugh at him: Lo, this is the man that made not God his strength; but trusted in the abundance of his riches, and strengthened himself in wickedness." (Psalms 52:6,7)
5. "Trust not in oppression, and become not vain

in robbery: if riches increase, set not your heart upon them." (Psalms 62:10)

6. "And they say, How doth God know? and is there knowledge in the most High? Behold, these are the ungodly, who prosper in the world; they increase in riches. Verily I have cleansed my heart in vain, and washed my hands in innocency. For all the day long have I been plagued, and chastened every morning. If I say, I will speak thus; behold, I should offend against the generation of thy children. When I thought to know this, it was too painful for me; Until I went into the sanctuary of God; then understood I their end. Surely thou didst set them in slippery places: thou castedst them down into destruction. How are they brought into desolation, as in a moment! they are utterly consumed with terrors. As a dream when one awaketh; so, O Lord, when thou awakest, thou shalt despise their image." (Psalms 73:11-20)

7. "Riches profit not in the day of wrath: but righteousness delivereth from death. . . . He that trusteth in his riches shall fall: but the righteous shall flourish as a branch." (Proverbs 11:4,28)

8. "Wilt thou set thine eyes upon that which is not? For riches certainly make themselves wings; they fly away as an eagle toward heaven." (Proverbs 23:5)

9. "There is a sore evil which I have seen under the sun, namely, riches kept for the owners thereof to their hurt. But those riches perish by evil travail: and he begetteth a son, and there is nothing in his hand." (Ecclesiastes 5:13,14)

10. "Behold, thou art wiser than Daniel; there is no secret that they can hide from thee: Wilt thy

wisdom and with thine understanding thou hast gotten thee riches, and hast gotten gold and silver into thy treasures: By thy great wisdom and by thy traffick hast thou increased thy riches, and thine heart is lifted up because of thy riches: Therefore thus saith the Lord God; Because thou hast set thine heart as the heart of God; Behold, therefore I will bring strangers upon thee, the terrible of the nations; and they shall draw their swords against the beauty of thy wisdom, and they shall defile thy brightness. They shall bring thee down to the pit, and thou shalt die the deaths of them that are slain in the midst of the seas." (Ezekiel 28:3-8)

Scriptures for Chapter Two

1. "For nation shall rise against nation, and kingdom against kingdom: and there shall be famines, and pestilences, and earthquakes, in divers places." (Matthew 24:7)

2. "For nation shall rise against nation, and kingdom against kingdom: and there shall be earthquakes in divers places, and there shall be famines and troubles: these are the beginnings of sorrows." (Mark 13:8)

3. "And great earthquakes shall be in divers places, and famines, and pestilences; and fearful sights and great signs shall there be from heaven." (Luke 21:11)

4. "The first angel sounded, and there followed hail and fire mingled with blood, and they were cast upon the earth: and the third part of trees was burnt up, and all green grass was burnt up." (Revelation 8:7)

5. "And the temple of God was opened in heaven, and there was seen in his temple the ark of his testament: and there were lightnings, and voices, and thunderings, and an earthquake, and great hail." (Revelation 11:19)

6. "And there fell upon men a great hail out of heaven, every stone about the weight of a talent: and men blasphemed God because of the plague of the hail; for the plague thereof was exceeding great." (Revelation 16:21)

7. "The floods have lifted up, O Lord, the floods have lifted up their voice; the floods lift up their waves." (Psalms 93:3)

8. "They did eat, they drank, they married wives, they were given in marriage, until the day that Noe entered into the ark, and the flood came, and destroyed them all." (Luke 17:27)

9. "But the men marvelled, saying, What manner of man is this, that even the winds and the sea obey him!" (Matthew 8:27)

10. "Daniel spake and said, I saw in my vision by night, and, behold, the four winds of the heaven strove upon the great sea." (Daniel 7:2)

11. "For he commandeth, and raiseth the stormy wind, which lifteth up the waves thereof." (Psalms 107:25)

12. "He causeth the vapours to ascend from the ends of the earth; he maketh lightnings for the rain; he bringeth the wind out of his treasuries." (Psalms 135:7)

13. "Fire, and hail; snow, and vapours; stormy wind fulfilling his word." (Psalms 148:8)

14. "Who hath ascended up into heaven or descended? who hath gathered the wind in his fists? who hath bound the waters in a garment? who hath established all the ends of the earth? what

is his name, and what is his son's name, if thou
canst tell?" (Proverbs 30:4)

Scriptures for Chapter Three

1. "And the serpent cast out of his mouth water
   as a flood after the woman, that he might cause
   her to be carried away of the flood. And the
   earth helped the woman, and the earth opened
   her mouth, and swallowed up the flood which
   the dragon cast out of his mouth." (Revelation
   12:15,16)

2. "The chariots shall rage in the streets, they
   shall justle one against another in the broad
   ways: they shall seem like torches, they shall
   run like the lightnings. He shall recount his
   worthies: they shall stumble in their walk; they
   shall make haste to the wall thereof, and the
   defence shall be prepared. The gates of the rivers shall be opened, and the palace shall be dis-
   solved." (Nahum 2:4,5,6)

3. "There is a generation that are pure in their
   own eyes, and yet is not washed from their
   filthiness." (Proverbs 30:12)

4. "But they also have erred through wine, and
   through strong drink are out of the way; the
   priest and the prophet have erred through
   strong drink, they are swallowed up of wine,
   they are out of the way through strong drink;
   they err in vision, they stumble in judgment.
   For all tables are full of vomit and filthiness, so
   that there is no place clean." (Isaiah 28:7,8)

5. "When thus it shall be in the midst of the land
   among the people, there shall be as the shaking

of an olive tree, and as the gleaning grapes when the vintage is done." (Isaiah 24:13)

6. "And the woman was arrayed in purple and scarlet colour, and decked with gold and precious stones and pearls, having a golden cup in her hand full of abominations and filthiness of her fornication:

And upon her forehead was a name written, MYSTERY, BABYLON THE GREAT, THE MOTHER OF HARLOTS AND ABOMINATIONS OF THE EARTH." (Revelation 17:4,5)

7. "God looked down from heaven upon the children of men, to see if there were any that did understand, that did seek God. Every one of them is gone back: they are altogether become filthy; there is none that doeth good, no, not one." (Psalms 53:2,3)

8. "And delivered just Lot, vexed with the filthy conversation of the wicked." (II Peter 2:7)

9. "Likewise also these filthy dreamers defile the flesh, despise dominion, and speak evil of dignities." (Jude 1:8)

10. "He that is unjust, let him be unjust still: and he which is filthy, let him be filthy still: and he that is righteous, let him be righteous still: and he that is holy, let him be holy still." (Revelation 22:11)

Scriptures for Chapter Four

1. "Think not that I am come to send peace on earth: I came not to send peace, but a sword. For I am come to set a man at variance against his father, and the daughter against her mother,

and the daughter in law against her mother in law. And a man's foes shall be they of his own household. He that loveth father or mother more than me is not worthy of me: and he that loveth son or daughter more than me is not worthy of me." (Matthew 10:34-37)

2. "There is a generation that curseth their father, and doth not bless their mother. . . . The eye that mocketh at his father, and despiseth to obey his mother, the ravens of the valley shall pick it out, and the young eagles shall eat it." (Proverbs 30:11, 17)

3. "When my father and my mother forsake me, then the Lord will take me up." (Psalms 27:10)

4. "A wise son maketh a glad father: but a foolish man despiseth his mother." (Proverbs 15:20)

5. "The rod and reproof give wisdom: but a child left to himself bringeth his mother to shame." (Proverbs 29:15)

6. "For God commanded, saying, Honour thy father and mother: and, He that curseth father or mother, let him die the death. But ye say, Whosoever shall say to his father or his mother, It is a gift, by whatsoever thou mightest be profited by me; And honour not his father or his mother, he shall be free. Thus have ye made the commandment of God of none effect by your tradition." (Matthew 15:4,5,6)

7. "And, ye fathers, provoke not your children to wrath: but bring them up in the nurture and admonition of the Lord." (Ephesians 6:4)

8. "Fathers, provoke not your children to anger, lest they be discouraged." (Colossians 3:21)

9. "For the time will come when they will not endure sound doctrine; but after their own lusts

shall they heap to themselves teachers, having itching ears." (II Timothy 4:3)

10. "Reprove not a scorner, lest he hate thee: rebuke a wise man, and he will love thee." (Proverbs 9:8)

11. "Who hate the good, and love the evil; who pluck off their skin from off them, and their flesh from off their bones." (Micah 3:2)

12. "And then shall many be offended, and shall betray one another, and shall hate one another." (Matthew 24:10)

13. "For he flattereth himself in his own eyes, until his iniquity be found to be hateful." (Psalms 36:2)

14. "For we ourselves also were sometimes foolish, disobedient, deceived, serving divers lusts and pleasures, living in malice and envy, hateful, and hating one another." (Titus 3:3)

Scriptures for Chapter Five

1. Blessed are they which are persecuted for righteousness' sake: for theirs is the kingdom of Heaven. Blessed are ye, when men shall revile you, and persecute you, and shall say all manner of evil against you falsely, for my sake. Rejoice, and be exceeding glad: for great is your reward in heaven: for so persecuted they the prophets which were before you." (Matthew 5:10,11,12)

2. "And the brother shall deliver up the brother to death, and the father the child: and the children shall rise up against their parents, and cause them to be put to death. And ye shall be hated of all men for my name's sake: but he that endureth to the end shall be saved. But when they

persecute you in this city, flee ye into another: for verily I say unto you, Ye shall not have gone over the cities of Israel, till the Son of man be come. The disciple is not above his master, nor the servant above his lord. It is enough for the disciple that he be as his master, and the servant as his lord. If they have called the master of the house Beelzebub, how much more shall they call them of his household?" (Matthew 10:21-25)

3. "If ye were of the world, the world would love his own: but because ye are not of the world, but I have chosen you out of the world, therefore the world hateth you. Remember the word that I said unto you, The servant is not greater than his lord. If they have persecuted me, they will also persecute you; if they have kept my saying, they will keep yours also." (John 15:19,20)

4. "We are troubled on every side, yet not distressed; we are perplexed, but not in despair: Persecuted, but not forsaken; cast down, but not destroyed; Always bearing about in the body the dying of the Lord Jesus, that the life also of Jesus might be made manifest in our body. For we which live are alway delivered unto death for Jesus' sake, that the life also of Jesus might be made manifest in our mortal flesh." (II Corinthians 4:8-11)

5. "But as then he that was born after the flesh persecuted him that was born after the Spirit, even so it is now." (Galatians 4:29)

6. "Yea, and all that will live godly in Christ Jesus shall suffer persecution." (II Timothy 3:12)

7. "Beloved, think it not strange concerning the fiery trial which is to try you, as though some strange thing happened unto you: But rejoice, inasmuch as ye are partakers of Christ's suffer-

ings; that, when his glory shall be revealed, ye
may be glad also with exceeding joy. If ye be re-
proached for the name of Christ, happy are ye;
for the spirit of glory and of God resteth upon
you; on their part he is evil spoken of, but on
your part he is glorified." (I Peter 4:12-14)

Scriptures for Chapter Seven

1. "Whereby are given unto us exceeding great
   and precious promises: that by these ye might
   be partakers of the divine nature, having es-
   caped the corruption that is in the world
   through lust." (II Peter 1:4)
2. "I will both lay me down in peace, and sleep:
   for thou, Lord, only makest me dwell in safety."
   (Psalms 4:8)
3. "But whoso hearkeneth unto me shall dwell
   safely, and shall be quiet from fear of evil."
   (Proverbs 1:33)
4. "The beloved of the Lord shall dwell in safety
   by him; and the Lord shall cover him all the
   day long, and he shall dwell between his shoulders." (Deuteronomy 33:12)
5. "The name of the Lord is a strong tower: the
   righteous runneth into it, and is safe." (Proverbs 18:10)
6. "As an eagle stirreth up her nest, fluttereth over
   her young, spreadeth abroad her wings, taketh
   them, beareth them on her wings: So the Lord
   alone did lead . . ." (Deuteronomy 32:11)
7. "And who is he that will harm you, if ye be followers of that which is good?" (I Peter 3:13)
8. "When thou passest through the waters, I will
   be with thee; and through the rivers, they shall

not overflow thee: when thou walkest through the fire, thou shalt not be burned; neither shall the flame kindle upon thee." (Isaiah 43:2)

9. "Many are the afflictions of the righteous: but the Lord delivereth him out of them all." (Psalms 34:19)

10. "Thou art my hiding place; thou shalt preserve me from trouble; thou shalt compass me about with songs of deliverance." (Psalms 32:7)

11. "God is our refuge and strength, a very present help in trouble." (Psalms 46:1)

S-17